THE
LITTLE
HISTORY
OF
COVENTRY

THE
LITTLE
HISTORY
OF
COVENTRY

PETER WALTERS

For Ellie and Pippa. The future.

First published 2019

The History Press
97 St George's Place, Cheltenham,
Gloucestershire, GL50 3QB
www.thehistorypress.co.uk

British Library Cataloguing in Publication Data.
A catalogue record for this book is available from the British Library.

ISBN 978-0-7509-8908-4

Typesetting and origination by The History Press
Printed in Turkey by Imak

CONTENTS

ABOUT THE AUTHOR

Peter Walters is not a native of Coventry, but has lived in the city since 1979. A journalist for many years, then a city promotions manager, he now divides his time between writing and engaging in a wide range of community activities. This is his third book on the history of Coventry and he's an active member of many local organisations, from the Coventry Society to the Tudor Coventry Group.

ACKNOWLEDGEMENTS

I would like to thank the following for their help in bring-ing this book to life: Stewart Ferguson, Chris Patrick, Martin Roberts, David Fry and Victoria Northridge. I also wish to record my thanks to Jill Belcham for allowing me to use the work of her late father, Robert Overy.

INTRODUCTION

If becoming the UK's City of Culture in 2021 does anything for Coventry, it ought to dispel the notion that the city that sits astride the centrefold of England is a shadowy, dull place that has contributed very little to the nation's story.

Once a medieval boom town, with a hotline into the centres of royal power, it was a key player in the dynastic wars of the fifteenth century and then a focus for dissent in the age of King versus Parliament.

Slumbering in its venerable street pattern over much of the next 200 years, it then took a wild lurch in a new direction, as first bicycles, then motor cars, took the place of its traditional staple industries, weaving and watch-making.

As the only place in this country forced to make the leap straight from the end of the Middle Ages into the twentieth century, Coventry rapidly outgrew itself, becoming by turns a high-wage economy for the working man and then an unemployment trap as whole industries deserted it in the 1980s.

To paraphrase the city's most famous cultural export, the poet Philip Larkin, 'it wasn't the place's fault', but in being forced to grapple with fundamental change time and time again, Coventry somehow lost its sense of identity, forfeiting the continuity that other historic cities in this country have enjoyed.

And yet. The city's uncanny ability to reinvent itself in the direst of circumstances is resurfacing again in the post-industrial world in which it now finds itself. Its two success-ful universities are the principal dynamos of an economy shorn of the manufacturing giants that once shaped it, but better balanced for the challenges ahead.

Even the severe and unadorned architecture of its post-1945 rebirth, universally mocked for two generations, is now suddenly in fashion and on trend. The next chapter in its thousand-year story looks intriguing.

1

OUT OF THE
SHADOWS

In his magisterial county history *The Antiquities Of Warwickshire*, Sir William Dugdale was uncharacteristically coy about the origins of Coventry. 'I am content to leave the period of obscure beginnings unexplored,' he wrote, 'confessing that I have so little of story to guide me through these elder times.'

Dugdale was writing in 1656, but more than 350 years later, that cautionary note still sounds. We are still unable to pin down with any certainty when, how or even exactly where this place had its beginnings.

That human beings have populated this well-watered and gently undulating corner of central England for millennia is not in doubt. In 2002 archaeologists identified an Iron Age village comprising at least seventeen dwellings on the campus of the University of Warwick, to the south-west of modern Coventry. Within the last decade, excavations to the south-east of the city, on the site of Orchard Retail Park, have thrown up an iron linchpin and horses' teeth from what is believed to be a late Iron Age chariot burial.

Roman roads criss-cross this part of the country, with Fosse Way and Watling Street passing to the east and north, less than 10 miles from Coventry. Yet the Lunt, the first-century auxiliary fort at nearby Baginton, remains the only significant Roman site in the vicinity.

Evidence from farmstead sites has been found in Coventry city centre, while Roman coin hoards discovered over the past couple of centuries close to what's now the Foleshill Road hint at an ancient trunk road, passing over a river crossing right at the heart of the modern city.

In 1933, local archaeologist John Shelton found the contents of a Roman lady's satchel in the River Sherbourne at Cox Street, complete with rings and toilet items for nails and ears. Yet if there was a settlement, perhaps gathered around that river crossing, in the centuries before Rome pulled out of Britain, its whereabouts have so far remained elusive.

A SAXON TOWN

The Domesday survey, that great Norman inventory of plundering possibilities, characterises Coventry as a scattered rural community, in which perhaps 300 people scratched a living from a large expanse of arable land, using twenty ploughs, and controlled a substantial area of woodland, covering about 2 square miles.

Yet that is literally less than half the story. The consensus among historians now is that by the late Saxon period, just before the Conquest, Coventry was a modest-sized town with a population of around 1,200 and, almost certainly, its own minster church.

The number of Old English 'ley' word-endings in local place names, denoting a clearing in woodland, would suggest settled occupation going back much further, on the edges of what now appears to us as the legendary, almost supernatural Forest of Arden. There's evidence that Arden as a dense, continuous woodland of the sort beloved of big screen outlaws, had receded by Roman times. But the Saxon settlers and farmers who followed still clearly associated their new homeland with

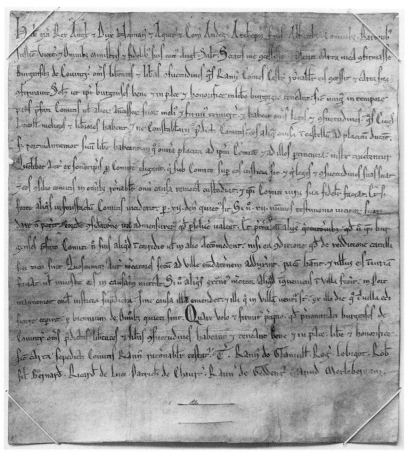

A sample from Domesday Book. (The History Press)

tree-clearing, and places like Allesley, Binley and Keresley are still classified as part of Coventry's ancient Arden landscape.

Pottery finds from an archaeological dig in the Palmer Lane area of the city centre, as recently as December 2017, have given new impetus to the theory that the earliest Anglo-Saxon settlement was there, close to the river. They were supported by the remarkable discovery of a stone causeway, with plant material on its surface still flattened into layers by the trampling of livestock, perhaps being driven to market, more than a thousand years ago.

WHAT'S IN A NAME?

Over the past century of scholarship a number of contenders have emerged. Could the name 'Coventry' have its origins in an ancient description of physical features in the landscape, principally a hillside and a cave? Or might it stem from the Roman water goddess Coventina, based on the tradition that the Roman general Agricola established a camp on Barrs Hill, north of the river, and set up a shrine nearby?

Increasing evidence for a settled, mature community around that river, centuries before the Norman Conquest, has, however, persuaded modern thinking that the city's name is much more likely to have its roots in the identity of a local Saxon landowner, Cofa, and a tree that marked the extent of his lordship.

We know nothing of Cofa himself, but trees were often used as boundary markers or objects of sacred veneration by the Saxons, and Cofa's tree might simply have been the mightiest of many. Recent archaeology has identified oak woodlands stretching right down to the north bank of the river, where Coventry's transport museum now stands.

ST OSBURG

Cofa might possess the naming rights, but was a woman actually the earliest known person with Coventry connections?

Her name was Osburga ('Osburg' in modern parlance). She was in religious orders and was reputed to be one of the nuns who left their house at Barking in Essex towards the end of the seventh century to found their own monastic settlements.

Osburg was abbess, it was said, of a nunnery established close to the River Sherbourne, and a reference to that foundation appears in some flyleaf jottings on a bound set of anonymous sermons, dating from the late fourteenth century:

> In ancient times on the bank of the river called by the inhabitants Sherbourne, which flows right through the centre of Coventry, there was formerly a monastery of young women dedicated to God.

Osburg remains a shadowy figure; she was later canonised but we know little more about her than that. The fate of her nunnery is a rather better known element of this old story. It was destroyed, the chroniclers recorded, in 1016 when a Danish army led by Canute, on his way to seizing the throne of England, ravaged Warwickshire.

While no hard evidence for that cataclysmic event has yet been unearthed, there are tantalising glimpses of a Danish presence in the area. Scandinavian names are surprisingly common among the inhabitants of twelfth- and thirteenth-century Coventry, while the city's Hock Tuesday play, performed on the second Tuesday after Easter from around 1416 until the early years of the seventeenth century, was said to owe its origins to celebrations of victory in battle against the Danes.

St Osburg herself certainly lingered in Coventry's collective memory. A shrine to her was established in the later cathedral of St Mary, and her head, enclosed in copper and gilt, was listed as one of its most important relics. In 1408, the Bishop of Coventry and Lichfield, John Burghill, responding to public pleas, ordered that her feast day of 30 March should be celebrated in the city.

A MINSTER CHURCH?

St Osburg's head was not the only relic of a cadaver housed in the cathedral. In 1022, Archbishop Aethelnoth, while in

Rome to be formally installed as Archbishop of Canterbury by Pope Benedict VIII, purchased a holy relic, the arm of St Augustine of Hippo. The chroniclers say that he paid 100 silver talents and one gold talent for it, and, more importantly, that on his return to England he gave it to the church in Coventry.

Whether that was a building associated with St Osburg's nunnery or, as many historians now believe, a Minster church for the growing community, is still open to question.

No foundation charter or documentary evidence exists for a Saxon minster at Coventry, but burials found during major excavations on the site of the first cathedral, St Mary's, in the early 2000s have been carbon-dated in the range of AD 700 to 980. There is also a further indicator in the location of the cathedral itself.

Very unusually, it does not lie at the top of what is now known as Hill Top, but on a site falling away to the north. The reason for that must be that there was already an ecclesiastical building of some kind at the summit of the hill, where Holy Trinity now stands.

The failure by the Domesday compilers to register the greater part of the Saxon town, in size perhaps similar to Warwick, is not unique. There are plenty of towns known to have existed at the time that do not feature at all in the Domesday survey, the ancient city of Winchester being an example. What was recorded of Coventry by the inventory clerks, it's now believed, was merely its rural hinterland.

LEOFRIC AND GODIVA

Whatever came before them, there is no dispute that in the year 1043, Leofric, Earl of Mercia, and his wife Godgifu (Godiva to us) came to an agreement with the Benedictine order to dedicate a house of abbot and twenty-four monks at Coventry.

A stained-glass image from the Benedictines' great cathedral. Could this be Godiva? (Continuum Group)

Neither could claim local antecedents. Godiva's origins remain obscure, although a fourteenth-century reference indicates that she was sister to Thorold, Sheriff of Lincolnshire, and may have spent her early life in that part of eastern England.

Leofric was probably born in the 990s, the third son of Leofwine, Ealdorman of the Hwicce, a Saxon tribal grouping that held sway over much of Worcestershire and south Warwickshire. Both his elder brothers had died in war, and in the maelstrom of pre-Conquest politics it may have suited him to establish a foothold in Coventry, in a corner of Mercia fairly distant from his own power base.

History has downplayed the importance of Leofric in the story of eleventh-century England. A protégé of Canute, he was one of a triumvirate of earls (Godwin of Wessex and Siward of Northumbria were the others) who held the ring in the turbulent years that followed the end of Danish rule in England in the early 1040s.

On his death in 1057, the eulogies described him as devout and illustrious, while the *Anglo-Saxon Chronicle* paid tribute to him as 'very wise in all matters, both religious and secular'. He was buried, the chroniclers agree, in a side chapel of his new abbey church of St Mary in Coventry, a foundation richly endowed with more than twenty estates, spread not only across Warwickshire, but Northamptonshire and Cheshire as well.

GODIVA'S RIDE

For all his achievements, Leofric plays a subsidiary and brutish role in the story that persists, almost a thousand years later, of the saintly Godiva's legendary ride to free the people of Coventry from unjust taxation.

That the real Godiva, who died ten years after her husband, was beautiful and of a saintly disposition seems plausible – all the stories that emerged later agree on that point. That she rode naked through the streets to free the people of taxes imposed by the 'grim earl' is, however, pure myth.

The tale, which emerged some 150 years after her death, owes something to the northern European pagan fertility rite that pairs a naked woman and a horse, and a lot more to inventive Benedictine monks keen to promote their Coventry foundation and highlight the sanctity of this most appealing of benefactors. Peeping Tom, the hapless tailor struck blind for daring to take a look at those long white legs, is an even later invention, from the sixteenth century.

Godiva's status (she was the only female Saxon landowner to be named in the Domesday survey) would not have permitted her to make a public gesture of that kind, and in any event, it was she who owned the lands on which the beginnings of Coventry were emerging and therefore would be the recipient of taxes raised from the inhabitants.

Nevertheless, the legend of the saintly Godiva and her selfless gesture became embedded in Coventry imaginations. More than once during the centuries that followed her death the townsfolk summoned up her example to assert their defiance when they felt themselves threatened by powerful interests.

Although she had a place in the Great Fair processions of the late Middle Ages, perhaps surprisingly, the good lady was not their central figure; another character from local myth, the dragon-slaying patron saint, St George, took precedence.

That changed, however, in 1678, when those with commercial interests in the town, fearing competition from a fast-emerging Birmingham, decided that she, not old St George in his armour, would attract the crowds. She was played that year by a boy, the young son of one James Swinnerton, but by the nineteenth century the role was taken by actresses, whose enthusiasm for the part, among the ribaldry of the crowds, often brought out senior clergy in a rash of condemnation.

Alfred Lord Tennyson went back to the chaste Godiva for his poem *Godiva*, written after he had made a railway excursion to Coventry in the early 1840s. Words from his poem were used on the imposing statue of Godiva, unveiled by the wife of the United States Ambassador to Britain in Broadgate in 1949.

More recently, this thousand-year-old icon has given her name to the annual summer Godiva Festival in Coventry and to Godiva's Day, which falls on 10 September, the supposed date of her death in 1067. The day celebrates selfless compassion and social justice, themes that still resonate in the modern world.

In 2012, she was given new shape in a 20ft-high animatronic figure that made its way, by cycle power, to London for the Olympic Games. There she represented the West Midlands region in the cultural Olympiad, under the banner 'Godiva Awakes'.

The myth endures.

2

THE EARLY TOWN

Whatever the true scale of Coventry at the time of the Domesday Book, we know almost nothing about the lives of the people who called it home in the early years of Norman rule. There are reasons for that. Coventry seems to have been particularly unlucky, or neglectful, in preserving the written record of its early history. Henry VIII's brutal dissolution of the monasteries at the end of the 1530s tore the heart out of the town and destroyed documentary evidence, both monastic and secular, by the cartload.

A catastrophic fire in Birmingham Library archives in 1879, and Second World War bomb damage, compounded these losses, and it has to be said that the preservation of heritage has not always been given high priority by those who have shaped Coventry in the modern world.

More importantly, Coventry's rise to become one of England's richest and most powerful towns happened fast and late. The boom town of the late fourteenth century was only just beginning to make its mark on England by the middle of the thirteenth century. As the *Victoria County History of Warwickshire* somewhat snootily put it, 'there is little evidence for the social history of Coventry before the fourteenth century'. This is not quite true, but life in the decades after the Conquest remains largely a shadow play, except for the poisonous and, to our eyes, astonishing chapter of conflict among those supposed to be doing God's work in these parts.

BISHOPS VERSUS MONKS

The dispute had its origins in the new Anglo-Norman administration's desire to see a bishop, operating in a clearly defined see, or diocese, take precedence over a monastic foundation, however powerful and well-endowed. From the start, Coventry's Benedictine Abbey was certainly that. The Benedictine chronicler John of Worcester, writing nearly a hundred years later, claimed that Leofric and Godiva had 'endowed it adequately with lands and made it so rich in various ornaments that in no monastery in England might be found the abundance of gold, silver, gems and precious stones that was at that time in its possession'.

Yet its location made it geographically part of the Mercian see, with its episcopal centre at Lichfield, and in 1075, Lanfranc, Archbishop of Canterbury, muddied the waters still further when he ordered that the see should be moved from modest Lichfield to the much bigger town of Chester, whose imposing foundations had been laid on top of the original Roman legionary fortress.

Lanfranc's reasoning – that a diocese should be based in a significant urban centre rather than a small town that was little more than a village – was sound. But it was a move that the Benedictine monks of Coventry would quickly come to regret.

ROBERT DE LIMESEY

Enter the first real villain in Coventry's story: the rapa-cious Robert de Limesey, a former chaplain to William the

A Benedictine monk from the eleventh century. (Image courtesy of the Thomas Fisher Rare Books Library, University of Toronto)

Conqueror with powerful connections to the heart of government, who was consecrated Bishop of Chester in 1086. Within a couple of years, Archbishop Lanfranc was ordering de Limesey to relieve the burdens he had imposed on the monks at Coventry and restore what he had taken from them. He had been accused of breaking into the monks' dormitory by force, with armed men at his back, wrenching open their strong box, and stealing the contents, as well as horses and other goods.

Worse was to come. Chester, close to the troublesome Welsh Marches, was proving a little too turbulent for de Limesey's taste, and in 1102 he successfully petitioned Pope Paschal II to move the see back to the Midlands, not to modest Lichfield, but to well-endowed Coventry. The move instantly turned the Abbey of St Mary into a cathedral, downgraded the Benedictine abbot to prior, and more importantly, brought their tormentor much closer to the monks.

The twelfth-century chronicler and historian William of Malmesbury, admittedly himself a Benedictine, did not mince his words in his judgment of de Limesey. The bishop, he claimed, was an embezzler who had stolen treasures from the abbey church, scraping from one beam supporting a shrine, silver worth a hefty 500 marks (at a time when a mark was worth two-thirds of a pound).

Moreover, he had allowed abbey buildings to collapse, spending money instead on his own projects, possibly including a new bishop's palace. He had fed the monks inferior victuals and deprived them of learning so that they were unable to oppose his wishes.

Whatever the truth of these allegations, de Limesey clearly sprang from that branch of the Anglo-Norman clergy who believed that a comfortable life in this world was no barrier to salvation in the next. When he died in 1117, his bishopric was left vacant for four years, much to the relief, no doubt, of those persecuted Benedictines.

THE BENEDICTINES IN COVENTRY

We know very little about the daily lives of these monk-ish Coventrians. While other Benedictine foundations like Evesham managed to preserve their early records, Coventry did not, almost certainly because at the Dissolution Henry VIII's commissioners put a match to them. We do, however, know what the monks looked like, thanks to a description that has come down to us from one of Coventry's later historians, Sir William Dugdale:

> A black coat, loose and divided down to their heels, with a cowl or hood that is shorter than others use. Underneath a white woollen coat, a hair shirt, with boots to the knees and heads shaved with a razor on top, called a corona.

The religious life they lived was intense. Every few hours, throughout the day and night, they were expected to attend services of formal worship. Study and contemplation filled many more hours, but while salvation of the soul was paramount, the Benedictines were far from an unworldly order. Skills of administration and business acumen were much prized, while their instinct for self-preservation was always fierce and could be highly developed. In some circumstances they were experts at being economical with the truth. It was the monks at Coventry who almost certainly invented the story of Lady Godiva's legendary naked ride, a century and a half after her death, to promote their own connections to such a saintly benefactor.

Very few of Coventry's early charters, said to have been secured by the monks, have turned out to be genuine, and many have one thing in common. They give the Benedictines full licence to pursue their interests, in trade or religion, free from outside interference. But to the order must go the credit for establishing a market at the gates of its priory, the cornerstone of Coventry's rise to become one of England's wealthiest and most important towns.

THE EARLS OF CHESTER

If the Benedictines had been instrumental in kick-starting the growth of an identifiable, urban Coventry, it was another Anglo-Norman force, this time secular, that gave it real acceleration. Hugh d'Avranches, first Earl of Chester, had acquired the estates once held by Godiva in the 1080s, but over the next forty years neither Hugh nor his successors paid much attention to their landholdings in Coventry, a tiny patch of ground in a fiefdom that ranged right across England and France.

However, the fourth earl, Ranulf II, who succeeded to the earldom in 1129, took a different view. As a military figure of some note, Ranulf had a keen sense of strategy and clearly saw Coventry as important to his family's future. Almost the first thing he did, possibly as early as 1130, was to begin work on some form of castle – little more, perhaps, than a fortified mound. Its exact whereabouts have remained a mystery to this day, yet place names in modern Coventry's city centre clearly speak of a fortification – Broadgate, Bayley Lane, Castle Yard and even Hay Lane (from 'haeg', meaning enclosure, not fodder for livestock).

Ranulf also seems to have erected a small chapel, later rebuilt in the fourteenth century as the imposing St Michael's Church, on the northern edge of his bailey, very close to the Benedictines' own small chapel, first recorded in 1113 and also later reconstructed as Holy Trinity Church. With hindsight, this looks like the opening move in the struggle between the priors and their secular rivals that split the emerging town into two halves and characterised its growth before the fourteenth century.

RANULF'S CHARTER

For the townsfolk, the presence of such powerful competing interests must have offered the prospect of burgeoning

prosperity, particularly as it was beginning to give Coventry
a regional profile as a place of some potential. That optimis-
tic view was no doubt reinforced by Ranulf's assignment to
those inhabitants, possibly as early as the 1140s, of a grant of
liberties conferring rights that in effect marked the beginnings

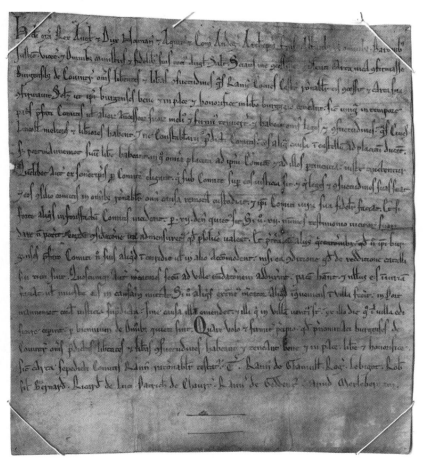

Henry II's charter of 1182. (Image courtesy of Culture Coventry
(Coventry Archives))

of civic government for the town. In it, the earl states that the burgesses of Coventry may hold their property in free burgage, allowing them to pass it on to their heirs, and that they should have their own court ('portmanmote') in which to settle disputes between themselves and the earl. They would be able to elect one of their number to represent them in their dealings with the earl. They would have the right to bring before the court errant merchants and could expect security for any loans made to the earl or his men. Furthermore, new investors in the town would be exempt from charges and taxes for two years, from the date they began building.

Nearly forty years later, Ranulf's grant was to be confirmed in a charter, formally signed off by Henry II at Marlborough in early 1182, that survives as possibly the earliest of Coventry's founding charters to be free of the taint of forgery.

At the time, Ranulf's grant of liberties appears to have had an immediate impact. There is evidence that Coventry's population showed a marked increase around the middle of the twelfth century, and the earl's inward investment incentives can take credit for that.

THE ANARCHY

Sadly, the rumble of civil war was already approaching to interrupt the hopes and dreams of those newly enfranchised burgesses. It was later dubbed the Anarchy, but was in essence a power struggle between Henry I's daughter Matilda, and her cousin Stephen, Count of Mortain.

As Henry's only surviving legitimate offspring, Matilda had a compelling claim to the throne. Through her mother, she also had Anglo-Saxon royal blood in her veins, a distinction that her enemies among the Norman nobility were quick to seize upon, contemptuously nicknaming her Godiva. Stephen, Henry's favourite nephew, could not match that claim to the throne but was an energetic and capable soldier, widely admired for his intelligence and generous disposition.

An engraving of Matilda's rival Stephen, being taken prisoner. (The History Press)

By 1140, the cat-and-mouse game the cousins were playing, all shifting alliances, skirmishes and feints, was coming
to a crunch. At this moment, Ranulf, Earl of Chester, having
taken his time to weigh up the strength of both parties,
declared for Matilda. He laid siege to Lincoln Castle, captured Stephen when he turned up with an army to lift the
siege, and, basking in the plaudits of a grateful Matilda,
appeared to have backed the winning side.

In the two years that followed, however, the tide slowly turned
in Stephen's favour, and by 1144 it was he who wore the crown,
albeit somewhat precariously, with neither side able to land the
decisive blow. In September of that year, one of Stephen's supporters in the Midlands, Robert Marmion, Earl of Tamworth,
decided to attack Ranulf's castle in the heart of Coventry.

Marmion, the warlike scion of a proud military family, once
champions to the dukes in their native Normandy, seized the
partly constructed buildings of the great new cathedral, begun
by the hated Bishop de Limesey nearly fifty years before, and
turned the site into a fortified camp from which to lay siege to
the earl's castle, no more than a stone's throw away.

Unfortunately for Marmion, he managed to forget where
he had dug some new defensive ditches in front of his lines
and, while riding out on a solo reconnaissance one day, fell
into one and was unhorsed. Rendered helpless by a broken
thigh, he was promptly dispatched with a knife by a humble
foot soldier – or, some even said, a cobbler.

Despite the loss of their commander, Marmion's small force
did manage to eject Ranulf from his castle. What exactly this
meant for the townsfolk, forced to pay helpless witness to
events beyond their control, is hard to say, although there is
evidence from a later charter that places of refuge were created for the poor during the fighting.

Three years later, Ranulf laid siege to the castle but was
beaten off and almost captured when Stephen himself came
to the rescue of its defenders. It was to be another seven
years, with Stephen, Matilda and Ranulf all dead, before

the new king, Henry II, returned Coventry's fortification to Ranulf's successor as Earl of Chester.

PEACE AND PROSPERITY

After the mayhem of the civil war, the 1150s would prove to be a decade of rapid growth for the emerging Coventry, largely thanks to a newly arrived commercial force, wearing the habits of monks but possessed of true money-making skills. In 1150, the Cistercian order, an austere offshoot of the Benedictines, who preferred a life of manual labour and self-sufficiency to the worldly sophistication of their mother order, established the beginnings of an abbey at Coombe, 5 miles to the east of Coventry. Five years later, they added another, 4 miles to the south, at Stoneleigh.

Medieval sheep farming. (Image courtesy of the Thomas Fisher Rare Books Library, University of Toronto)

The Cistercians were permitted to own property as a way of keeping body and soul together, and within a remarkably short time had major property holdings in the town. But they possessed another great attribute that could unlock the key to real wealth in the early Middle Ages – they were *the* great experts at farming sheep.

As their two abbeys began to establish an almost industrial production line in wool, they needed a market through which to sell it. Coventry's market, created by the Benedictines around a century before, was perfectly placed. The Benedictine priors themselves, however, were far from idle. The shrewd and powerful Prior Lawrence, who was elected to the post in 1149 and stayed in it for thirty years, has a good claim to be regarded as one of the key founders of early Coventry.

Prior Lawrence recommenced work on the great cathedral church, begun by Bishop de Limesey, which was rising on the site of the modest foundation established by Leofric and Godiva. In 1155 he gave land 'between the two bridges' (or Burges, as we now know it) on which to build the hospital of St John, offering temporary relief and lodging to poor wayfarers and permanent relief for up to twenty poor folk in Coventry who were old and sick.

The hospital, whose fourteenth-century chapel survives as the oldest standing building in central Coventry, was the first institution to undertake active social work in the town and was in itself something of a statement. Coventry was now big enough and of sufficient interest to visitors and those engaged in trade to warrant such a hospital.

Even more remarkably, it was an unprecedented example of priory and diocesan clergy working together. While Prior Lawrence gave money to build the hospital, the driving force behind its construction was Edmund, Archdeacon of Coventry and one of the bishop's right-hand men – usually viewed as sworn enemies of the Benedictines.

HUGH NONANT

This outbreak of peace between cowl and mitre was not destined to last. The dispute rumbled on through the succeeding decades, flaring up each time a new bishop was chosen, generally not a candidate the other side would support.

Gerald la Purcelle, who became bishop in 1183, was a renowned diplomat and master of canon law and might have been able to breach the divide, but he died after just a year in office – poisoned, it was whispered, but almost certainly just overcome by age. The man who followed him into office in 1185 was every Benedictine's worst nightmare come true. Hugh Nonant had also been a diplomat and was unable to take up his post until 1188, as he was on royal business abroad.

Nonant was almost certainly given the bishop's mitre as a reward for his service, and set about making himself comfortable, purchasing the office of Sheriff in Warwickshire, Leicestershire and Staffordshire and acquiring the rights and possessions of Coventry Priory by paying the new king, Richard I, a bribe of 300 marks for his Crusader war chest.

As if this wasn't enough, Nonant was a man with a hatred of monks that bordered on the pathological. 'I call my clerks (the canons of Lichfield) gods and the monks demons,' he was reputed to have said, adding that if he had his way he would 'strip every cowled head in England'. When he declared his intention to move the episcopal chair from Coventry to Lichfield and began calling himself Bishop of Coventry and Lichfield, the blue touch paper flared. In a replay of the controversies surrounding Robert de Limesey, a century earlier, he was accused of breaking into the priory with armed men and ejecting the monks, installing a community of canons from Lichfield in their place and giving away priory property as bribes for papal officials to turn a blind eye to what he was doing. Nonant, in his turn, complained to the Pope that he had been physically assaulted by the monks, smashed over the head with a crucifix during a struggle in the cathedral church itself. Then there was the tale that whilst supervising the ongoing building works, he had narrowly escaped being brained by a huge block of stone that had mysteriously detached itself from a high wall above, killing a young monk standing next to him.

In 1196, the venal Nonant retired to the Abbey of Bec in Normandy, ironically one of the greatest Benedictine houses in France, where he begged the order for forgiveness and repented a list of sins so long, it was said, that nobody could be found to absolve him. He died two years later, after a long and painful illness (thoroughly merited in the eyes of a vengeful Benedictine chronicler).

REBELLION AGAIN

The great cathedral church of St Mary may have been rising steadily above the small town of Coventry, but time was running out for its castle. In 1173, Hugh Kevelioc, fifth Earl of Chester, joined the rebellion against Henry II, was captured and narrowly escaped execution. As penance, the king ordered that many of his castles, including Coventry, should be slighted, or damaged beyond repair. From this point on it begins to slip away into history.

By the time of his death in 1181, Hugh had left one positive legacy to Coventry – a leper hospital and chapel dedicated to St Mary Magdalene. No traces of it remain, but its memory lives on in the name of the suburb that later grew up around the area it stood in, to the west of the town: Chapelfields.

A DEVELOPING TOWN

Earl Hugh's rebellious instincts had cost the citizens of Coventry dear. Fines were levied on them for trying to conceal from confiscation lands that belonged to Henry II's enemies, and in the end it cost them 200 marks to recover their fragile liberties from the Crown. Yet during the years that followed, the template for the city that would eventually emerge was beginning to be laid out.

From the market outside the gates of the rising cathedral church, Bishop Street struck north over the River Sherbourne towards Barrs Hill and Tamworth, and Lichfield beyond. Further south, on an east–west axis, the beginnings of Gosford Street and Spon Street flanked a central area, dominated by Smithford Street (the king's highway) and the thoroughfare called Earl Street.

The people who lived in this straggle of streets, lined with wooden houses, still laboured on the land; the imprints of oxen hooves from ploughing, laid on the ground more than a century after this period, have been found beneath fourteenth-century buildings in Gosford Street. Yet they were starting to acquire other skills, and it is at this time that the ordinary Coventrians begin to appear in the records. Among the first is Liulf de Brinklow – judging by his name, clearly an immigrant to the town – who in the 1150s is recorded as holding properties in Coventry in free burgage from the Earl of Chester. Liulf may well have been an official working for the earl, and he was clearly intent on putting down strong roots in his new community. By the 1220s, his family had acquired a substantial urban estate of fifteen 'messuages' (dwellings) and a chamber. Another recent immigrant, Alice de Corley, appears in a transaction from the year 1200 as the owner of a messuage in the market area, 'before the door of the Prior of Coventry'.

The market itself was developing, solid wooden structures replacing makeshift shelters as stalls for the growing number of traders attracted from some distance around. There's evidence too that separate timber and cattle markets were established in Bishop Street and Cook Street by the year 1203, and that the first of Coventry's mills, Hill Mill, was already operating, fed by the Radford Brook, close to what is now Naul's Mill Park.

The commercial life of the town received a further boost in 1218, when the men of the earl's half were granted the right to hold an eight-day fair and market, effectively the beginnings of what would become the renowned Coventry Great Fair. Nine years later, the Benedictine prior Geoffrey purchased from the king the right to hold his own annual three-day fair in October.

By the 1220s, the Cistercians at Coombe Abbey were well on their way to becoming the biggest property investors in Coventry, building a close working partnership with the emerging class of merchants who could market their wool. The people with whom they were keen to deal were now taking on surnames that reflected the trades and crafts they were practising. The early records from around 1200 name Ralph the weaver, Alexander the quareur (quarryman), Pagan the miller, Ailwin le furner (charcoal-burner) and John le brocher (thatcher). Among them, too, were Coventrians ready to supply what might be regarded as the finer things in life – Adam le vinetur (vintner or wine merchant) and Geoffrey the goldsmith. For the town to boast a goldsmith, there must already have been personal wealth to support his business. Coventry's golden age was just beginning to dawn.

FROM THE BACKS OF SHEEP

Wool was one of the most important currencies of wealth in medieval England, and Warwickshire wool was highly prized for its quality. The Cistercians may have been the great sheep experts but the Benedictines were also substantial producers, managing huge flocks on their granges, or farms, in the countryside surrounding the growing town.

Until the 1250s, the trade in wool dominated Coventry's commercial life, with fleeces being exported all over England

and even abroad, making fortunes for many of the families involved. But as early as 1200 the making of cloth was already on the increase, its techniques almost certainly introduced by immigrants from the eastern counties of England where skills had been learned from the Continent.

The trade was to receive a huge boost early in the fourteenth century, when the purchase of cloth for the Royal Wardrobe, effectively a government department, was switched from abroad to domestic markets, notably Coventry's. By 1345, the incorporation year for the town, a drapery (or market hall for the assessment and sale of cloth) was operating in Bayley Lane. Within fifty years it was dealing with 3,000 whole cloths annually, enough work to give a living to eighty weavers and their families, working a two-handed horizontal loom.

AN ELEPHANT AND A CASTLE

The earliest surviving image of Coventry's highly distinctive civic regalia comes from a circular seal, dated around 1250, which depicts an elephant bearing a triple-towered castle on its back and standing in front of an oak tree. A century later, the motif was almost certainly adopted as the centrepiece of the newly incorporated town's civic crest. But why choose an elephant?

Nobody in medieval Coventry had ever seen a real elephant, but they were known from the 'Bestiaries', books of fabulous beasts, whose activities and characteristics were used to highlight human qualities and frailties. The elephant represented strength and purpose, slaying a dragon to protect its young, but it was also believed to lean against trees as it slept and could be rendered defenceless when the tree was chopped down. Was the castle on its back an attempt to bolster that weakness, or to evoke memories of the Earl of Chester's 'modest fortlet' in Coventry? We shall

Coventry's elephant and castle. (Image courtesy of Culture Coventry (Coventry Archives))

probably never know. Nevertheless, the elephant and castle as a distinctive 'badge' for the town was highly valued and was increasingly used as a mark of quality, stamped on all of Coventry's cloth as it found its way into markets right across Europe.

3

A GOLDEN AGE

On 26 October 1232, Ranulf de Blondeville, sixth Earl of
Chester, died at his castle at Wallingford in Oxfordshire. He
was the last of his line, and his death brought to an end the
long and generally fruitful relationship between the earls
and Coventry.

Ranulf had shown a steady and personal interest in the town.
His charter of the early 1200s had reinforced the liberties given
to his tenants in Coventry by his grandfather, the fourth earl,
half a century before. Another grant, from around 1204, had
confirmed the rights of the Benedictine priory to take wood
from his extensive woodlands for fuel and building repairs.

In 1226, he had sought, and received, consent from King
Henry III to offer formal protection to the small Jewish communities of Coventry and Leicester, a move almost certainly
prompted by a series of bitter court cases, in which Amtera,
the Jewess of Coventry, successfully secured the forfeiture
of lands by debtors who had failed to pay back her loans
to them. Her victory no doubt fuelled hatreds among those
local debtors and it is surely no coincidence that after the
earl's death, Coventry's small community of Jews seems to
have moved elsewhere.

Ranulf himself was known for his willingness to repay his
debts to Jewish moneylenders, and one of the projects for which
he may well have needed their finance was the building of a
fortified manor house to replace the 'modest fortlet', slighted

by King Henry II, that he had inherited from his rebellious father. Cheylesmore Manor, begun possibly as early as 1206, was built at the town end of his hunting park, surrounded by a moat. Its timber-framed gatehouse, largely dating from the fourteenth century, survives as Coventry's register office.

Recent research into Coventry's development as a town has suggested that Ranulf may even have gone further, beginning to lay out the area between what is now Little Park Street and Much Park Street, in what was perhaps the first example of deliberate urban design in Coventry.

THE FRANCISCANS

For all his secular pursuits, Ranulf's most far-reaching legacy for Coventry may well have been his decision in 1231, a year before his death, to invite the Franciscan order to establish a friary on the doorstep of his new Cheylesmore Manor. The Franciscans, or Greyfriars as they were better known in England, were a mendicant order of street preachers, who preferred to rely for their sustenance on the generosity of well-wishers rather than the money-making schemes favoured by the more worldly monastic orders.

To the Benedictines, the Greyfriars' humility and simple lifestyle felt like a direct challenge, but what really grated was their popularity when it came to presiding over burials. For many rich and powerful people, a simple interment by the Greyfriars, shorn of high ceremony and the accoutrements of wealth, quickly became the preferred route to salvation in the next world.

The Greyfriars' new Coventry friary, its modest church roofed with wooden tiles thanks to a special grant of timber from Ranulf's estates, was to become its most important outside London. For 300 years it offered a final resting place to generations of the high-born and well-to-do from Coventry and Warwickshire, and even from the capital itself.

A STONE TOWN

If the Greyfriars, at least at the outset, were content to build in wood, others were already moving on to stone. By the early 1220s, the Cistercians at Coombe had completed their own new church, built in stone from their Harnall quarries, north of the town. Around the same time, the Benedictines were putting the finishing touches to their great cathedral church of St Mary, a building that in the course of its century-long construction had evolved in design from Romanesque at its east end to Early English at the west end.

Stone was becoming the building material of choice, too, for the emerging new class of wealthy merchants and crafts-men who were succeeding the Earls of Chester as leaders of a community that now numbered some 3,500 souls. They started to build more of their houses in stone, particularly around Well Street and West Orchard in the prior's half of the town, and they began to cluster together in identifiable quarters – smiths, dyers and weavers around Smithford Street, saddlers and goldsmiths along Broadgate, scabbard-makers and cutlers in Little Park and Much Park streets.

This confident new property-owning class numbered men like Henry Baker. As his name suggests, he came from a family with roots in a fairly humble occupation, but from the 1250s he began to amass an impressive portfolio of properties right across the town, from Bishop Street to Much Park Street.

To protect their growing stake in Coventry, Henry and his fellow prominent citizens began to think a little more about defending themselves, adding bars or chains on the main approaches to the town to strengthen the rubbish-clogged ditches that had once served as crude defences. Yet it would be the enemy within who would threaten to interrupt their steady march towards prosperity and civic stability.

Medieval houses in High Street, painted around 1820 by William Henry Brookes. (Image courtesy of Culture Coventry (Herbert Art Gallery and Museum))

THE ENEMY WITHIN

Ranulf, Earl of Chester's Coventry estates had passed in line through his nephew to one of his sisters, whose husband, Roger de Montalt, decided to join the Seventh Crusade in 1249 and, finding himself short of funds to do so, was persuaded by the entrepreneurial Benedictine prior, William de Brightwalton, to sell all his Coventry holdings, except Cheylesmore Manor, the house of the Greyfriars and the leper hospital founded by the fifth Earl of Chester.

At a stroke, the Benedictines found themselves taking control over the part of Coventry they had long coveted, and it wasn't very long before they took steps to consolidate their grip on the commercial life of the town. In February 1267, by charter of Henry III, the prior was granted the right to appoint a coroner, and more importantly, to set up for his tenants a guild merchant – a formal association that gave them privileges and exclusive rights to trade. In effect, this shut out many of the traders and craftsmen from the earl's half of the town. There was going to be trouble.

Rioting flared on the streets and the crisis reached a flashpoint when the Sheriff of Warwickshire, the king's official representative in the county, was called in to restore order and his clerk set out to investigate. A later report recorded what happened next:

> Certain men from these parts (the earl's half), with others, armed with force, took Gilbert, clerk to the said sheriff, sent hither to this end, and imprisoned him, and broke the royal rolls and charters and beat and ill-treated the men of the prior and convent.

The protest, in part at least, seems to have been successful. While the office of coroner was established and continued in Coventry, nothing more was heard of the prior's guild merchant. What is even more surprising is that the perpetrators of the assault do not appear to have felt the full weight of judicial retribution.

A PLACE OF INTEREST

It is conceivable that Coventry's rising profile as a town on the move may have aided those involved in defying the sheriff. Its sharply increasing prosperity was just beginning to be noticed in royal circles, where it truly mattered.

In 1285, King Edward I gave the townsfolk the authority to take a toll from all saleable commodities brought into the town to pay for paving the streets. The toll amounted to one halfpenny for every horse-load of corn and every horse, mare, ox or cow entering Coventry, and when the cash raised didn't prove sufficient, the king was happy to issue another licence.

Coventry had not been invited to send representatives to the rebel Simon de Montfort's groundbreaking parliament of 1265, but in 1295, two of its burgesses, Aunketil de Coleshull and Richard de Weston, did go to Edward I's Model Parliament, in effect becoming Coventry's first Members of Parliament. Six years later, two more Coventry merchants, Thomas Ballard and Lawrence de Shepey, were summoned by the king to a council at York, convened specifically to raise money for his war against the Scots, and in the years that followed, Coventry burgesses were included on every invitation list to councils where the king was seeking loans from wealthy subjects.

By this time, Coventry boasted more goldsmiths than Leicester or Nottingham and had a higher percentage of merchants in its population than Norwich, already England's second largest town. The list of trades active in Coventry included brooch makers, spice dealers, sewers of silk and dealers in venison and game, all occupations geared towards the luxury end of the market. The 'pavage' grant of 1285

further revealed that goods to be taxed included cloth of silk
with gold and baudekyn, a very expensive material used for
altar cloths as well as fashionable clothes.

A FATAL SOLUTION

Merchants and craftsmen involved in trades like these
had a lot to lose and deeply resented interference from the
Benedictine prior, now Coventry's undisputed landlord.
In Prior Henry de Leycester, elected in 1294, they found a
target worthy of their hatred. In 1302 and again in 1307,
de Leycester went to law to stop traders in the earl's half of
the town from selling goods from their own premises on the
days on which the market in his part of the town was being
held. He won, and his opponents found themselves facing a
substantial fine of £60.

De Leycester died in 1322, but his successor, Henry Irreys,
was no more sympathetic to the men of the earl's half. The
stage was set for a confrontation that resonates vividly
down the centuries. In December 1323, a group of powerful
merchants, led by Richard le Latoner, approached John de
Nottingham, a necromancer living with his assistant Robert
le Mareschal in a dilapidated old house in Shortley Park, close
to the town. Their proposal was brutal in its simplicity. Using
wax and canvas supplied by the merchants, Nottingham and
le Mareschal would employ sorcery to kill Irreys, his steward
Nicholas Crump, King Edward II, who had approved Irreys's
election, and the king's hated favourites Hugh Despenser and
his son, also named Hugh. The pair were told they would be
paid £35 to carry out this far-reaching attack.

An underling of the prior, Robert Sowe, who had probably made himself unpopular as well, was singled out as the
guinea pig for a trial run. A waxen image was made of him
and a sharpened pin driven into its heart. Within days he was
dead. At this point le Mareschal, a humble tailor by profes-

sion, panicked and confessed his part in the plot. John de Nottingham and a number of Coventry's most prominent and wealthy merchants were arrested by the Sheriff's officers and the case brought to trial in London.

The accused had the backing of fellow merchants in Warwickshire and in London – an indication, perhaps, of the resentment right across the country against the power of the monasteries. Yet, when the case came to trial in 1325, their help was not required. Rather conveniently, it turned out that John de Nottingham had died in jail and a jury promptly brought in not guilty verdicts for those in the dock. The report of the case, in the Parliamentary Writs, remains the earliest account of a witchcraft trial in England.

HERE COMES THE QUEEN

Despite the acquittals, the prospects for the Benedictine prior's opponents in Coventry looked pretty grim, until an astonishing stroke of luck presented itself. In 1327, Robert de Montalt, grandson of the man who had acquired Cheylesmore Manor eighty years before, drew up a deed, formally bequeathing it to Queen Isabella, widow of King Edward II, if he and his wife died without issue. Three years later that duly came to pass and Isabella was suddenly a force to be reckoned with in Coventry.

Supposedly 'in retirement', although in reality she had been exiled to Castle Rising in Norfolk by her son Edward III, Isabella took a keen interest in financial returns from her estates, including Cheylesmore Manor. Having spent a lifetime of intrigue with whole kingdoms at stake, a little local difficulty with a grasping Benedictine prior did not trouble Isabella overmuch, and she was to prove an ally without compare to the townsfolk.

In 1337 Prior Irreys complained to the king that 'Madame', as he called Isabella, had allowed her officers to seize profits from his fair. Furthermore, the people of Coventry had thrown down hedges and ditches in his park, run off 100 of his fattest cattle and 'attached and arrested' two cart-loads of corn being driven to the priory in broad daylight and in the middle of the street.

King Edward waved the protests away. He had already shown where his sympathies lay by in 1332 granting a licence for the men of the earl's half to erect a common conduit 20ft long and 10ft wide wherever they thought fit. In effect, it was Coventry's first public water supply, and from this moment on, the currents of history would shift away from the Benedictines in favour of the city's ambitious and acquisitive merchants and craftsmen. Eight years later, much against the will of the prior, they were given the right to establish a merchant guild of their own to protect their interests. St Mary's Guild, regarded initially as a focal point for opposition to the prior, was quickly followed by others: the Guild of St John the Baptist (1342), the Guild of St Katherine (1345), Corpus Christi (1348) and finally Holy Trinity Guild (1364), which, by the 1390s, had united all but Corpus Christi in its ranks.

BOOM TIMES

Coventry was moving rapidly up the list of England's most important towns; an assessment for tax in 1334 had rated it the twelfth wealthiest in the kingdom, equal to Salisbury, and it was on the threshold of an unprecedented building boom. Work on the Guildhall of St Mary, home to the first of the guilds, was nearing completion by 1342, and two years later Queen Isabella gave the Guild of St John the Baptist land at Bablake, on the western boundary of the town, to build a collegiate church where priests could live and study together, while singing the praises of their benefactors.

With paved streets, a public water supply and a new generation of imposing stone buildings, Coventry had reached a

St John's Church, drawn by Nathaniel Troughton in the early
nineteenth century. (Image courtesy of Culture Coventry (Coventry
Archives))

level of urban sophistication enjoyed by few other towns. The
stage was set for its next great leap in self-government. On
25 January 1345, Edward III granted the men of Coventry
favours and privileges, 'that they and their heirs and successors may henceforth have a commonalty [or corporation]
among themselves and may annually elect and create from
among themselves a fit Mayor and Bailiffs'.

It was a Charter of Incorporation, the first of a new kind
in England, supported in name by Queen Isabella herself and
negotiated, or 'purchased', by twelve prominent citizens:
Nicholas Mitchell, Henry Dodenhall, Walter Whitwebb,
Roger Hunte, Will Trymelei, Geoffrey Freebern, John
Rushall, Rob Thimbler, Will Walsall, Richard Keresley,
Maurice Norfolk and Will Wendiborough.

THE CARMELITES

In the same year that St Mary's Hall was preparing to open its doors, another monastic order was making its appearance in Coventry, wishing to take a stake in this increasingly attractive centre of both wealth and monasticism. The Carmelite order of friars, known as the Whitefriars because of the colour of their habits, owed this new foundation to the generosity of a private benefactor, the merchant Sir John Poulteney, four times Mayor of London. In 1342 he gave them 10 acres of land and a dwelling house close to what in time would become the London Road into Coventry. A further grant of land quickly followed from the Benedictine priory, a move perhaps designed to encourage the establishment of a rival order of mendicant street friars to the hated Greyfriars. The church they began building would be almost cathedral-scale in its ambition, with an impressive preaching nave, a slender tower and, unusually, resonance passages cut into the floor to improve the acoustics for singing.

THE BLACK DEATH

It is impossible to say when the plague reached Coventry. Even though the death rate really got into its stride in the spring of 1349, the disease may have been present in the town the previous autumn. The Benedictine prior William Irreys, who had succeeded his namesake Henry seven years earlier, was a victim that summer, as was Coventry's second mayor, Jordan de Shepey, and Richard Keresley, one of the twelve signatories to the Charter of Incorporation. Exactly what the death toll was, in a population of around 7,000, is hard to gauge, but it is likely that up to a fifth of all people in Coventry perished, the barely imaginable equivalent of more than 65,000 deaths among the city's population today.

Land remained uncultivated. Several of the town's mills, including Hill Mill, were left untended for want of a miller, and it was said that the majority of the prior's tenants, the heads of upwards of a hundred families in the farming areas of Exhall, Keresley, Willenhall and Coundon, had died. The impact of the disaster can be seen most clearly, and poignantly, in the property transactions for Coventry in 1349. John de Arthingworth, for example, was a wealthy Coventry merchant, appointed the first town coroner in 1346 and a property owner of some magnitude. He died of the pestilence in late March 1349, bequeathing his property, in part, to his widow Lucy and only daughter Joan. Yet by the middle of April young Joan's share had been passed on to her mother and she disappears from the record, clearly another victim.

The coming of the Black Death was to prove an early test for the fledgling merchant guilds, set up to protect and maintain their members just a year or two before. In the event, the guilds, through their trustees, became the repository of many properties from plague-ravaged families and played a vital role in fending off chaos.

RECOVERY

Just six years later, in 1355, Queen Isabella, the Benedictine prior (now William de Dunstable) and the new mayor signed the Tripartite Indenture, bringing to an end the disputes that had scarred the recent history of the town. In truth, the men of the earl's half had never quarrelled with their counterparts in the prior's half. It was the prior himself, and the power wielded by the Benedictines, that they had long opposed. At a time of crisis, the Indenture was intended formally to bind an emerging civic relationship even more tightly together.

In the same year, another great unifying force made its appearance in the townscape. Twenty-five years earlier, King Edward III had given the prior and the 'good men' of the town the right to levy 'murage', a tax to raise money to build a wall. In the summer of 1355, Richard de Stoke, Coventry's ninth mayor, finally laid the first stone, close to where the Carmelites had built their new friary.

The first mile took forty years to complete and it was to be almost 180 years before the town was completely encircled, but Coventry's town wall was to become one of the wonders of the late Middle Ages – 2¼ miles long, at least 12ft high, up to 9ft thick and furnished with thirty-two towers and twelve gates. Its tiny image appears, under construction, on the first modern map of England, dated around 1360.

Queen Isabella had made a further contribution to the expansion of the town, leasing quarter-acre plots of land to prominent citizens in the Little Park area of her estate, but it was left to her sub-bailiff in Coventry, William Walshman, to make the critical intervention that lifted Coventry into the ranks of England's most important towns.

With Isabella's strong backing, Walshman managed to prise the purchase of cloth for the Royal Wardrobe, virtually a government department, away from London to Coventry, giving the trade locally a huge boost. By 1377, when the tax assessors came to look at all of England's most important towns, Coventry was rated the fourth wealthiest, after London, York and Bristol. Remarkably, the population had recovered too, presumably fuelled by further immigration, to stand at around 9,000.

BUILDING IN STONE

The monastic jigsaw that was Coventry was finally completed in September 1385 when King Richard II and his young queen, Anne of Bohemia, laid the foundation stone of the Carthusian order's simple church at their new Charterhouse in the fields at Shortley, just south of the town. The king had already given the townsfolk the right to quarry stone from his

Cheylesmore estate for the new town wall, and Coventry's wealth was prompting others to build in stone too.

In the centre of the city, work was already underway to rebuild and expand the churches of Holy Trinity and St Michael's. In both cases, only a porch is thought to have survived from the earlier buildings as major works gave both churches something of the scale and appearance that survives today.

THE DUEL THAT NEVER WAS

In September 1397, King Richard again turned his attention to Coventry, choosing it as the venue for a trial by combat between his cousin, Henry Bolingbroke, Duke of Hereford, and Thomas Mowbray, Duke of Norfolk, one of his closest advisers. As Richard's reign had descended into paranoia and betrayal, each had accused the other of treason, and the resolution of their quarrel, devised by the king, was to be a duel to death on horseback, with lance and sword, on Gosford Green, a large expanse of open land beyond the walls to the east of the town.

As both men, gorgeously attired in their family colours and glittering armour, prepared to charge, however, Richard called a halt to proceedings, consulted his advisers, then banished Bolingbroke from England for ten years and Mowbray for life. It was to be the first public demonstration of family rivalries that would turn the century that followed into a nightmare of brutal atrocity and civil war. Mowbray died in exile, but within two years Bolingbroke was back to usurp the throne as Henry IV. Richard was captured at Lichfield, brought briefly to Coventry and then taken to London, where the following year he died in prison, almost certainly starved to death.

A nineteenth-century engraving of the duel that never was. (The History Press)

4

DARKENING SKIES

In early January 1394, a few days before the Feast of Epiphany, a triple murder stunned the prosperous and civic-minded community of Coventry. The bodies of John Cristleton, his son William and their servant Ralph Giffard were discovered in the sexton's house at the priory, where they lived. They had been hacked to death and robbed of a large sum in cash and jewellery worth a very tempting £10. The murderer, Geoffrey Wytles, was long gone, leaving behind him the murder weapon, an axe valued at 2*d*.

Crime had been a constant thread as the town developed, and Coventry's growing wealth put temptation in the way of many. In 1382, John Ray, an 'alnager', or collector of excise duty on cloth, was accused of a large-scale fraud against the king, by stealing 900 cloths brought to the Coventry Drapery for him to inspect and seal. We do not know what fate befell Ray, but the town did at least have its own machinery of justice in place, appointing its first Justices of the Peace in 1374 and a Recorder, or legal adviser, at roughly the same time.

THE LEET

The earliest surviving reference to the Leet – a legislative assembly, designed to replace the old feudal system of justice and draw up and enforce local by-laws governing life in the town – comes from 1384. It met twice a year, in January and September, with the mayor and bailiffs acting as presidents. It was the Leet that came up with the idea, in 1422, of inviting commoners to represent the ten wards of the town – Bayley Lane, Bishop Street, Broadgate, Cross Cheaping, Earl Street, Gosford Street, Jordan Well, Much Park Street, Smithford Street and Spon Street. It also first made reference to a town clerk in 1430 and to aldermen in 1469.

Its record of activity, the Leet Book, which survives from 1421 to the mid-1550s, is a fascinating glimpse of life in fifteenth- and early sixteenth-century Coventry, recording the creation of new by-laws on a whole host of civic concerns, from street cleansing and refuse disposal to protection of the water supply and the regulation of food prices.

The Leet ruled that no animals except pigs could be slaughtered within the town walls, that there would be fines for anyone caught sweeping rubbish into the river, and that householders should keep the pavement in front of their homes in good repair. Mindful of public safety and the appalling risk of fire, in 1474 it also threatened to come down hard on anybody who sought to build a thatched roof in the town.

More surprisingly, perhaps, the Leet also took an interest in how the children of Coventry were to be educated. The Benedictines had founded a school for the children of their tenants and officials as early as 1303, and there was another, run by the Carthusians at the Charterhouse, set up shortly after their arrival in Coventry in the 1380s. In 1425, the Leet appointed John Barton as master of a town grammar school and followed him in 1429 with a successor, John Pynchard. Ten years later it felt the need to chide the Benedictine priory for trying to force its tenants to send their children to the priory's school. A man, it decreed, could send his children to whichever school he wished. The ruling has a distinctly modern cast to it, but to describe the Leet as in any way inclusive or democratic would be wrong.

THE OLIGARCHY

The Leet lay at the heart of what was, in a very real sense, a self-perpetuating oligarchy. It appointed the mayor and bailiffs, but in turn its twenty-four members, or 'jury', were appointed by them. And they were all men who had been, or still were, prominent in trade and the Coventry guilds. A typical flight path for an ambitious man of affairs in Coventry might be master of the Corpus Christi guild one year, mayor the next, and master of the Trinity guild the next.

The mayor himself wielded formidable powers, aided by his council, numbering the twenty-four members of the Leet jury – known locally as The Scarlet, from the colour of their ceremonial robes – and a small number of close advisers, or 'brethren', who acted as an inner cabinet. With such power could come public exposure when things went wrong. In 1387, angry townsfolk stormed St Mary's Hall, already the headquarters of civic government in Coventry, and threw loaves of bread at the mayor, Henry de Keel, for not enforcing the rules that governed the quality and price of bread.

Three years earlier, the people of the town had objected to members of the powerful Trinity Guild taking control of four fields that were regarded as common land. The Leet ordered that men should be convened from every street in the town, sixty-eight in total, to decide what to do. They found in favour of the guild, but amongst their opponents the suspicion remained that these were merely placemen, acting in the interests of that powerful oligarchy who, through its membership of the most powerful guild in Coventry, ran the place. It would not be the last dispute over common lands between the ordinary citizens and those who ruled over them.

A PARLIAMENT IN COVENTRY

The wealth of Coventry's oligarchy and the importance of its Benedictine priory made it a natural focus of attention for the Crown, particularly when the treasury coffers began to ring hollow. In 1400, the financially hard-pressed King Henry IV borrowed a hefty sum of £300 from some of Coventry's most prominent merchants, never actually getting round to paying off £163 of it. Four years later, royal finances were again top of the agenda when Henry called a parliament in Coventry in early October 1404. It was called the Unlearned Parliament, as the king had forbidden lawyers from attending. It met in the great hall of the priory and the atmosphere was, to say the least, poisonous.

The Commons – the eighty-three knights and burgesses who represented the shires and towns – were bitterly resentful of the burden being placed on them, and argued that the Church was not contributing its share to the king's finances. Anti-clerical feeling was everywhere. When the Archbishop of Canterbury, Thomas Arundel, encountered a procession bearing sacramental bread to a sick man's bedside, he bent the knee in homage, and was outraged to see a group of the king's knights turn their backs on it, without even breaking off their conversation. 'Never before,' he raged, 'was the like abomination beheld among Christian men.'

The archbishop felt compelled to voice the threat of excommunication before the Commons would draw back from their preferred solution – confiscating revenues from Church lands for a year to meet the king's demands. In the end, after more than a month of debate, the Unlearned Parliament granted Henry IV the taxes he sought, with the proviso that war treasurers should be appointed to oversee spending in defence of the realm.

CHURCH VERSUS COMMONS

Divisions between the Church and the Commons, exposed on this national stage, rumbled on in Coventry. With so many important people in town, the parliament's host, the Benedictine prior, Richard Crosby, had hoped to raise the

The chapel of St George on Gosford Bridge, painted shortly before its demolition in the 1820s. (Image courtesy of Culture Coventry (Herbert Art Gallery and Museum))

damage done by townsfolk to a water conduit used by the priory, but his protests were waved away.

By this time, it is clear that the Benedictines increasingly viewed those they lived among as little more than a criminal rabble. By 1421, the prior was calling for a special watch to be kept on rowdy crowds who filled the streets during religious festivals.

Law and order seems to have been very much on the mind of the ruling class too. In the same year, the Leet forbade the carrying of weapons in the streets, a sensible precaution at a time when rough justice was still the first resort for many an injured party. Members of the oligarchy were also fearful of the power of new craft guilds, the earliest being the Guild of the Shearmen and Tailors, founded in the 1390s, followed within a decade by a weavers' guild and then a guild for dyers. When dissatisfied journeymen within those trades decided to set up a guild just for themselves, the Fraternity of St Anne, it was ruthlessly suppressed, by order of the Leet.

HENRY V AND COVENTRY

On 21 March 1421, the victor of Agincourt brought his young queen Catherine to Coventry and in a lavish ceremony the royal couple were presented with £100 in cash and each given a gold cup worth £10, which the merchants felt was a gift worthy of any royal visitor. It was to be the king's last visit to Coventry; he would die of dysentery the following year while on campaign in France. It is a fair assumption that his early passing would have been much mourned in the town.

There is some evidence that Henry V was a regular visitor to Coventry. In 1412, the year before he came to the throne, he was recorded as staying at the priory during a visit. In 1416, the year after Agincourt, he was again in Coventry, this time in search of funds. He borrowed 200 marks from the mayor and community, leaving in pledge his great Iklynton collar, garnished with 'four rubies, four great sapphires, thirty-two great pearls, and fifty-three other pearls of a lesser sort', and valued at £500. Presumably such an astonishing piece of royal regalia was in due course pretty swiftly redeemed.

MARGERY RUSSELL

When a loan to the king, or to important nobles, was agreed, the system dictated, somewhat bizarrely, that every man should make his contribution, ranging from 13*s* 4*d* taken from major property owners to a penny from men of the poorest classes. This rule was not just applied to men either, for there's plenty of evidence for independently wealthy women in Coventry at this time too. In 1412, Margery Russell from Coventry sought permission through the English courts to equip ships to hunt down and seize back goods worth a staggering £800 from Spanish merchants, after claiming that she had been robbed of a cargo worth that sum by pirates operating out of the Spanish port of Santander.

The formidable Margery, a member of the powerful Trinity Guild, was only one of a number of wealthy women active in trade in fifteenth-century Coventry, and in a town that owed much of its historical development to two women, Lady Godiva and Queen Isabella, and possibly even to a third, St Osburg, that seems only fitting. Their contribution to royal loans must have been significant.

THE LOLLARDS

Dubbed 'Lollards', or mutterers, by their enemies, they were regarded as dangerous heretics by the established monastic orders. And they owed their creed to a courageous and determined reformer based just 15 miles from Coventry. John Wycliffe, Rector of Lutterworth until his death in 1384, advocated the translation of the Bible into English and opposed corruption in the Church and the influence of the Pope and clergy over secular affairs. Support for his views in Coventry was strong – an echo, perhaps, of that long-running struggle in the town against the Benedictine prior, and that may well have been what persuaded the renegade priest John Ball to seek refuge in the town after the failure of the Peasants' Revolt in 1381.

Ball was arrested at an old, ruined house in the district of Whitley just outside Coventry, put on trial in his home town of St Albans and hanged, drawn and quartered. The following year, the Lollard preacher William Swynderby, known as William the Hermit, tried to preach in Coventry but was driven out by the clergy.

Another prominent Lollard, Nicholas of Hereford, a former pupil of Wycliffe, had translated part of the Old Testament for his old teacher, but had later recanted and for many years pursued his former colleagues as heretics. As an old man, he joined the community of monks at the Coventry Charterhouse, where he died in 1417.

Seven years later, in late November 1424, Lollardy showed its face again in Coventry in the shape of John Grace, a former monk and friar, who claimed he had permission from the bishop to preach for five days in Cheylesmore Park. Grace was a popular figure, admired for his saintly lifestyle and gifts as a speaker, and, to the horror of the Benedictine prior Richard Crosby, began to attract large crowds. Crosby and an unlikely ally, Friar John Bredon, master of the Greyfriars in Coventry, with whom the Benedictines had been at odds for nearly 200 years, set out to denounce Grace in Holy Trinity Church, but had to be rescued by the mayor, John Braytofte, after an angry crowd gathered threateningly in the churchyard.

In truth, there were many in Coventry who sympathised with Lollard ideals and supported them. In due course, Grace was arrested and ended up in the Tower of London, but the authorities in Coventry had been reluctant to move against him. The following spring, when sureties of good behaviour were demanded from around fifty Coventry artisans, that they would obey the mayor and not favour Lollardy, the orders came from London, not the Coventry Leet.

It was inevitable that in 1431, when a weaver, Jack Sharpe, led a rising against an unpopular Benedictine abbot in his home town of Abingdon in Berkshire, Coventry people would get involved. The rising's links to Lollardy were tenuous, to say the least, but in the wake of what the authorities chose to see as a dangerous rebellion, a number of Coventry folk followed Sharpe to the gallows, including a woman who was said to be the wife of a former mayor. Her identity remains a mystery, but she may have been the wife of wealthy mercer Ralph Garton, never mayor but a prominent Lollard sympathiser in the town.

ANOTHER KIND OF EARTHQUAKE

Right in the middle of all this religious ferment came an event that the God-fearing in Coventry would certainly have viewed as a sign of heavenly displeasure. On 28 September 1426, according to the City Annals:

> Between one and two in the morning, began a terrific Earthquake with lightning and thunder, and continued two hours. It was universal; men thought ye Day of Judgment was come. The beasts of the field roared and drew to the towns with hideous noises, and the wild fowls of the air cried out.

In the event, Coventry appears to have suffered no damage from the tremor, but it may well have prompted the creation of the 'Coventry Doom', a remarkable depiction of the Day of Judgment, painted high on the chancel wall of Holy Trinity Church by unknown local artists, early in the 1430s.

Uncovered and restored in the late 1990s, the painting was revealed to be almost complete and is now regarded as

The Coventry Doom. Was an earthquake the trigger for it?
(Holy Trinity Church)

perhaps the finest work of art of its kind to have survived
and one of the most important discoveries to have been
made in the field of medieval art. It teems with detail, showing sinners – including recalcitrant ale-wives who have been
watering the beer – being dragged by demons to the mouth

of hell, yawning open with huge fangs, while the godly rise
from their graves to sit at the right hand of God.

JOHN THORNTON

The quality of the Holy Trinity Doom painting suggests
another specialist Coventry craft from the late Middle Ages that
remains shadowy, but was to boast its finest exponent in John
Thornton, a glass painter born in the town, probably in the
early 1360s. Not much of his painted glass survives intact in his
native city, but his greatest work certainly does – the Great East
Window in York Minster, the biggest and generally regarded as
the finest work in stained glass in medieval England.

Thornton most likely secured his lucrative contract in
December 1405 through connections with Richard Scope,
Archbishop of York, who had been Bishop of Coventry and
Lichfield until 1398 and probably knew his work. After meeting his three-year deadline for the window, Thornton stayed
on in York, becoming a freeman of the city in 1410. He was
back in Coventry by 1413, with a workshop and house close
to the Burges, but later returned to York and was still living
there in the 1430s. Before heading north, Thornton may well
have designed the windows of the new church of St Michael
in Coventry, back in the 1390s. Surviving fragments certainly
betray his trademark style of white glass and yellow stain, set
against blue and ruby patterned backgrounds, and his highly
distinctive modelling of faces.

CIVIC PRIDE

While Coventry could not boast the cultural richness of York,
its own success as a wealthy centre of commerce had embedded a growing sense of civic pride and cultural ambition. In
1423 the Leet Book made its first reference to the 'waits' or

town band, recording the appointment of four musicians, led by a trumpeter and paid quarterly, who would be expected to play in the streets at night and on important occasions. Provided with rent-free cottages by the Trinity Guild and

Representation of a Pageant Vehicle and Play.

The state, and reverence, and show,
Were so attractive, folks would go
From all parts, ev'ry year, to see
These pageant-plays at Coventry.

A Coventry mystery play in performance. (Image courtesy of Culture Coventry (Coventry Archives))

dressed in coats of green and red, Coventry's ceremonial colours, they entertained with pipe, drum and strings at festivities of all kinds, becoming so sought-after that a later command of the Leet restricted them to making appearances at religious houses no more than 10 miles from Coventry.

The waits' most important task was to provide the soundtrack to the pageants, plays with a biblical framework performed by the craft guilds on the streets at the Feast of Corpus Christi in early June. There were ten of them in all, bringing to life New Testament stories, from the Annunciation to the Last Judgment, and over the next 200 years they would make Coventry's name famous and do wonders for the local visitor economy.

THE COMING STORM

In May 1448, bystanders witnessed 'a great affray' in the heart of the town between long-standing enemies Sir Humphrey Stafford and Sir Robert Harcourt and their retainers, in which a number of combatants, including Stafford's eldest son Richard, were killed. This was no ordinary brawl. Their feud reflected the taking of sides in the approaching conflict between the houses of York and Lancaster, first exposed to the light by the duel-that-never-was on Gosford Green, fifty years before.

In the general muster of the following year, designed to test Coventry's defences in time of war, the craft guilds raised 600 able-bodied men to defend the town, and in July 1450 it looked as though that state of readiness was about to be tested, when the Kentish rebel Jack Cade raised an army of 5,000 men and stormed and looted London. For a time it appeared as if the rebellion would spread, and the Leet deployed forty armed men to keep watch all night. Four brass cannons were hurriedly purchased from Bristol, then the country's leading centre for manufacturing iron, and mounted on the town walls at the new Bablake Gate. In the event, Cade's army never reached the Midlands, but his uprising had been a test for a man who was about to become very involved in Coventry's story. And it was a test he had failed.

HENRY VI

Henry VI had been an infant when his warlike father had died on campaign in France. After long years of regency he had finally come of age in 1445, being crowned king in May of that year, alongside his new young wife, the teenage but already strong-willed Margaret of Anjou. By 1450, his passivity as commander-in-chief had already cost England most of its possessions in France, leaving the country full of embittered, defeated soldiery, who blamed the king and his advisers for their plight and would prove a natural recruiting ground for the coming struggle. He'd also failed miserably to persuade Cade and his rebels to give up, fleeing back to his stronghold of Kenilworth Castle from where he began to seek fresh allies in the Midlands, beginning with what was still its most powerful town.

Henry arrived in Coventry in late September, greeted by the mayor and his brethren on the road from Leicester. He lodged at the priory and celebrated mass at St Michael's, his presence giving a royal seal of approval to the church's extraordinary new spire. He stayed for two weeks and on the day of his departure announced that he would confer the status of city and county on Coventry, divorcing it from Warwickshire in an administrative break-away that would endure until local government reforms of the early 1840s. A subsequent charter, issued on 26 November 1451, incorporated outlying settlements like Radford, Keresley, Foleshill, Coundon, Wyken, Stoke and Whitley into the new county and gave Coventry goods freedom from tolls, not only throughout England, but in Ireland as well. It was a city at last, but with its colours nailed firmly to the Lancastrian mast.

LANCASTER OR YORK

While pro-Lancastrian sentiment was strong in the new city, there was always a significant minority who favoured the Yorkists, gathered around the wealthy merchant quarter of Little Park Street and an inn called the White Rose, or Roebuck. When the king's mind gave way to some sort of catatonic illness in the summer of 1453, after news of a devastating English defeat in Gascony, it was Richard, Duke of York, who persuaded the lords to make him protector of the realm, against the queen's wishes.

By Christmas 1454, Henry had recovered his wits, but it was too late to prevent the first savage encounter of the Wars of the Roses, a bloody skirmish at St Albans in May 1455, in which Margaret's chief supporter, Edmund Beaufort, Duke of Somerset, was killed. Coventry men may well have fought on the Lancastrian side at St Albans, beneath the standard of the Black Ram, and when the king suffered a relapse in the months that followed, Queen Margaret decided that London was unsafe and that Coventry would serve better as an alternative centre of royal power.

THE QUEEN'S BOWER

The royal household arrived on 14 September 1456, greeted by the mayor and council bearing lavish gifts and a programme of carefully planned pageants, staged to compare Margaret to the queen of heaven. She was to spend so much time in Coventry over the next few years that the city became known as 'the Queen's bower'. In the following month, a 'Great Council' met in Coventry to try to find some common ground in a conflict that had already horrified contemporaries with its brutality. Richard, Duke of York, swore a public oath of allegiance to Henry, yet by the time Margaret moved on, in the spring of 1457, he had already refused to attend a second council in the city.

By early 1459, Queen Margaret was back in Coventry, this time with an army at her back. Richard of York and his nephew and right-hand-man Richard Neville, Earl of Warwick, failed to attend a third Great Council and fled abroad. At the parliament of 20 November, the second to be held in Coventry, York, Warwick and their chief supporters were declared traitors and 'attainted,' with their lives and property forfeit to the Crown. After the 'Devilish Parliament', as the Yorkists called it, there would be no going back.

STILL LANCASTRIAN?

By the following spring, unease at Margaret's abrasive rule and the idea of government from Coventry had begun to tip the scales in the Yorkist direction. York and Warwick landed back in England and defeated Margaret's forces at Northampton on 10 July 1460, making a captive of Henry, who was found quietly sitting in his tent while the battle raged around him. Five months later, York was killed at another furious encounter, this time at Wakefield. It was a seemingly decisive blow that turned out to be merely the latest grisly turn of events as England's ruling class tore itself to pieces.

In late 1465 it looked as though Coventry might come under siege as York's second son, now the clever and imposing Edward IV, advanced on the city with a force including 200 archers to arrest his erstwhile ally, the Earl of Warwick, and his own brother, George, Duke of Clarence, who had taken shelter within its walls. They were accused of treason but the charges were finally judged to be ill-founded, and all of them spent a convivial Christmas together in the city.

Six years later, Edward returned to blockade Coventry to force out Warwick, who, it turned out, had switched sides after all. Edward failed, but at the Battle of Barnet in March 1471, Warwick was killed and the final blow fell for the Lancastrians two months later at Tewkesbury, when Margaret's son Edward was killed in battle and the queen herself taken prisoner. She was brought to Edward IV at Coventry – 'the Queen's bower' no more.

FOR YORK

Edward mistrusted Coventry for its past support for the Lancastrian cause, on this visit confiscating the city's ceremonial sword and removing its liberties, which included a newly granted right to mint coinage. Within a year, he had restored those liberties, albeit at a handsome price of 500 marks. That he was willing to forgive, although never entirely trust, the city, owed much to the way in which those who ran it managed to adapt to the swirling fortunes of the conflict – men like John Smyth, a wealthy member of the Bakers Company, whose name first appears in the general muster of 1449.

Twelve years later, the Leet Book records him contributing to the military costs of the Earl of Warwick as he pursued the remnants of the Lancastrian army after their terrible defeat at Towton in Yorkshire. In 1468 he is among those helping to pay the cost of entertaining Elizabeth Woodville, wife of Edward IV, and in the next couple of years the records show him helping to pay the wages of Coventry men fighting in Edward's army in skirmishes at Exeter and Nottingham and contributing towards a loan offered to the king. In August 1485, however, just two days after the shattering defeat of the Yorkist cause at the Battle of Bosworth Field, John Smyth is among those hurriedly forking out for a feast to entertain the new king, Henry VII, at the house of the mayor, Robert Onley, in Smithford Street. Lancaster now is the house to which Coventry must once again pledge its loyalty.

5

A FANATIC TOWN

In March 1485, eight Coventry men – John Blomston, alias Master John the Physician, Richard Hegham, Robert Crowther, John Smith, Roger Brown, Thomas Butler, John Falkes and Richard Silwyn – were brought before John Hales, Bishop of Coventry and Lichfield, and accused of mocking the veneration shown to sites of pilgrimage in the city, notably the Whitefriars' chapel of Our Lady In The Tower. After confessing their guilt, the eight were made to walk barefoot from St Michael's Church to the market place, and then to the chapel in the wall, each carrying a faggot on their shoulder to symbolise the burning that surely awaited them if they transgressed again. It was a reminder that the heretical instincts of Lollardy, so strong in Coventry sixty years earlier, had not disappeared. It also chimed with a wider sense that the forces of anti-authoritarianism and dissent were on the march, epitomised by a serial rebel from the very heart of Coventry's oligarchy.

LAURENCE SAUNDERS

As the son of a former mayor and a member of both Holy Trinity and Corpus Christi guilds, the dyer Laurence Saunders was on the fast track to advancement in late fifteenth-century Coventry. His appointment, in early 1480, to one of the two posts of Chamberlain in the city ought to have been the first rung on the ladder to power and authority. Instead, to the horror of those who had nodded his appointment through, it triggered his first act of rebellion. Saunders and his fellow Chamberlain, William Hede, were tasked with responsibility for building and maintaining the town wall, as well as safeguarding the rights of the citizens when it came to the common lands. They refused to pay the wages of labourers working on the wall, as custom dictated, arguing instead that those who had set them to work should pay.

For this, they were confined to prison for a week and made to pay a substantial fine, but while Hede recanted, Saunders was soon being accused of levying excessive fines on those whose livestock had exceeded the quota permitted to graze on common land, notably a landowner named William Bristowe, who had already clashed with the Saunders family over the issue. Back in 1469, the year Laurence's father William had been mayor, Bristowe had built a wall enclosing what was widely considered to be common land at Whitley. In response, a crowd of up to 500 citizens (led, it was claimed, by the mayor himself) marched out of the city, tore down the wall and returned in high spirits, serenaded by the waits, playing triumphal airs.

This dispute had dragged on through the courts and now Laurence travelled privately to the Prince of Wales's Council at Ludlow to present a petition alleging that common lands were being withheld from the people in Coventry, while favoured landowners were given unrestricted access. His petition failed and he was jailed briefly, had to kneel before the mayor and council in St Mary's Hall to plead forgiveness, and was fined a hefty £15 11s 1d.

This didn't stop him, however. Two years later he was briefly jailed again after protesting loudly about enclosures. Forced to recant, Laurence was silent for more than a decade, but in August 1494 he was arrested again after urging a crowd in the marketplace to seize oats belonging to William Boteler, son of a former recorder, and treat them as their own. Flung into jail for seven months, he was stripped of all offices and membership of the guilds, and warned that he faced death if he persisted in fomenting rebellion. Two years later he petitioned the mayor, John Dove, demanding that enclosures should be stopped, and when that was rejected, threatened rebellion. In November 1496 his case was sent to the Star Chamber in London for trial and he was committed to the Fleet Prison to await the verdict.

That is the last historical record of Laurence Saunders. In all probability he died in jail, but the old rebel's story remains the fullest account of a municipal controversy to survive from the fifteenth century.

DECLINING FORTUNES

Turbulence in local politics and religious affairs was being echoed in an economy that had propelled the city to such eminence 100 years before. With the cloth trade in decline, it is estimated that the population of Coventry had fallen from a peak of around 10,000 earlier in the century to no more than 8,500. In 1485, the Holy Trinity guild, one of Coventry's most powerful landlords, reported that 135 of its 387 houses and cottages were empty.

In the final decade of the century, a new craft – using wool to make caps and other headgear – had been introduced, giving immigration a significant boost and ensuring that in the century ahead, cappers would enjoy a high profile in Coventry, with a number becoming mayor. Within twenty years, however, the bloom on that new industry had faded and the city was experiencing severe economic hardship. In April 1518, the Leet issued a desperate plea for craftsmen from elsewhere to settle in Coventry, promising that after a year they could secure the protection of one of the craft guilds, as long as they were prepared to pay the membership fees.

Poor harvests in 1518 and 1519 had been followed by the 'year of dearth' in 1520, when disease and even starvation threatened. The city was swollen with beggars from the countryside, fleeing abject poverty and finding little sympathy among Coventry's ruling oligarchy, who ordered that 'those lying in the fields, breaking hedges and stealing fruit' should be expelled forthwith.

THE FIRST CENSUS

An unprecedented snapshot of those living in Coventry at the time comes from a remarkable document, the earliest surviving census of a town in England. It was commissioned in the autumn of 1520 by the mayor, John Bond, and included population figures for each of the city's ten wards as well as a breakdown of occupations – revealing, for example, that there were sixty-eight brewers and forty-three bakers at work in the city. Its total population reckoning of 6,600 seems on the low side, but reflects the straitened circumstances in which Coventry now found itself.

LIFE IN THE TOWN

For the ordinary citizen living in Coventry at the turn of the sixteenth century, life was relatively short, often brutish and always tightly controlled by the governing elite. The day-bell was rung at 4 a.m. from St Michael's and Holy Trinity, at which the night watch stood down, the city gates were opened and the water conduits unlocked. By 5 a.m., unemployed craftsmen had to be at the city's central crossroads (Smithford Street and Broadgate), ready for hire if needed. For most people, the working day began around 6 a.m. and routinely lasted for fourteen hours, with surprisingly modern-style breaks built into it. At the end of the working day, curfew was sung in the central churches at 8 p.m., the city gates were locked an hour later and the lanterns that hung outside inns and the houses of the better-off had to be extinguished.

Strict regulations governed the basic transactions of daily life. Corn could be sold at market on Monday, meat and hides on Tuesday. On Wednesday, the mayor and council would receive petitions from fellow citizens about concerns and disputes and it was also the day on which bakers were allowed into the city to sell their wares. Meat was again available at market on Thursday, while on Friday, the chief market day of the week, fish, corn and bread could be sold and the drapery, or cloth market, operated. Saturday, which was payday for most people, was the only day of rest, on which a working man could resort to an alehouse or, if he belonged to the right guild, to one of the city's more upmarket inns: the Cardinal's Hat in Earl Street, perhaps, or the Crown in Broadgate. Sunday, of course, was meant to be a day of contemplation and religious observance, although before that the streets had to be swept clear outside every tenement, ready for inspection by the city aldermen, who at all times were tasked with keeping a constant eye out 'for all them that keep misrule'.

KEEPING MISRULE

This might mean frequenting 'blind' or secret inns – where who knows what went on – or indulging in unlawful pursuits like 'roving': firing arrows at targets while on the move. The sport had been outlawed, probably on safety grounds, since 1468, when by specific command of King Edward IV, butts had been set up at which people could practise their skills at archery. Fines were imposed for playing bowls or quoits in city streets. Brawling was expressly forbidden and there were serious concerns about the rowdiness of celebrations that attended Coventry's festive calendar, notably the feasts of Midsummer Eve and St Peter's Eve in the autumn, when houses were decorated in greenery, neighbours caroused in the streets and bonfires were lit in every ward.

PHILANTHROPY LIVES

In 1509, the wool merchant William Ford, who had been mayor in 1497, died and left money in his will to build an

Ford's Hospital, still in use as a home for the elderly. (Image from the work of Robert Overy, courtesy of Jill Belcham)

almshouse on land belonging to the Greyfriars. Initially, it would house five elderly men, with a woman to look after them and a stipend of 5*d* a week, but Ford's bequest was later added to by a capper, William Pisford, who introduced another of his own, leaving money to give thirteen poor maidens 20*s* each when they married.

Wealthy draper Thomas Bond, who had been mayor of Coventry the year after Ford, had in 1506 bequeathed money to found another almshouse, this time for ten elderly men, with a woman to look after them, close to the collegiate church of Bablake. Another draper, John Haddon, in his will dated 1518, left £100 to be divided into loans for young cloth-makers pursuing his own trade, and a further £100 in loans for the use of struggling craftsmen in other trades. Whether these acts of charity were motivated by anything more than empathy for their fellow citizens remains unproven, but it is true that even among the elite, the creed of Lollardy was very much alive in Coventry.

LOLLARD MARTYRS

The first Coventry follower to suffer the ultimate penalty for her faith was Joan Ward, who had admitted to being a Lollard back in the 1490s, recanted and moved away from the city. On her return in 1511, however, she once more adopted her old beliefs. She was condemned as a relapsed heretic and went to the stake on 12 March 1512. Eight years later, on 4 April 1520, seven further Lollards followed her to the execution ground, in a hollow in what had been King Richard II's old quarry in the park at Cheylesmore. Thomas Bond, Hosea Hawkins, Robert Hachett and John Archer were shoemakers, Thomas Landsdale was a hosier and Thomas Wrigsham a glover.

The seventh, widow Joan Smith, was initially discharged but was brought back for trial after an official escorting her home discovered an English translation of the Lord's

The Martyrs' Mosaic, a modern tribute to those who went to the stake in Coventry. (Image courtesy of Culture Coventry (Coventry Archives))

Prayer and the Ten Commandments hidden in her sleeve. An eighth Coventry Lollard, the sect's librarian Robert Silkeby, had also been arrested, but escaped. He was captured some eighteen months later and on 13 January 1522 he too paid a horrifying price for his heresy.

JOHN RASTELL

In such a climate of fear and economic uncertainty, it's not surprising that many members of Coventry's ruling families were beginning to look elsewhere for their future, because the city could no longer accommodate their ambitions. One such was John Rastell, the son of a magistrate, born around 1475 into a Coventry family that had long been active in city affairs. Lawyer, printer, dramatist, designer, reformer and cosmographer, Rastell was perhaps the closest a native Coventrian has ever come to being a true renaissance man.

Although much of his remarkable career was achieved in London, its roots lay in Coventry. Sworn into the Corpus Christi guild while still in his teens, Rastell trained as a lawyer and in 1507 was appointed coroner for Coventry.

Rastell's horizons had already extended beyond the city with his marriage, some time before 1504, to Elizabeth More, sister of Thomas More, Henry VIII's future Lord Chancellor and, eventually, martyred saint. There is evidence, however, that he retained close connections with his birthplace, acting as paid adviser to his guild and helping to stage pageants performed in Coventry as late as 1510.

From 1508, Rastell appears as a printer in London, becoming possibly the first in Europe to print a musical score. He had also become a lawyer of the Middle Temple, a position that may have been brokered by Thomas More. When war with France broke out four years later, he was working for Sir Edward Belknap, brother of Henry VIII's Clerk of Works, and played a modest role in the conflict, overseeing the transport of guns.

Rastell was profoundly influenced by the utopian ideas of his brilliant brother-in-law, and in search of a living embodiment of that utopia, he joined an expedition to the New World in the summer of 1517, possibly to help found a colony. Once afloat, the ship's master declared that he preferred to 'go robbing on the seas' and put Rastell ashore in Ireland. No doubt infuriated by this experience, later in the year Rastell wrote and published a morality play, *The Nature of the Four Elements*. In 1520, he was tasked with designing the lavishly decorated temporary buildings for Henry VIII's celebrated meeting with the King of France at the Field of the Cloth of Gold, a precursor to a series of pageants he was to devise for the king in the years that followed.

In 1524, Rastell built himself a house in Finsbury Fields in London, complete with its own theatre, for which he would write and direct plays and masques, while his wife made and hired out theatrical costumes. Fifty years later it became the first public stage in London.

In the last decade of his life, Rastell emerged as a pro-lific writer and publisher on law; at least one of his works is still in use. Having been a staunch Catholic for most of his life, he became a passionate supporter of reform, work-ing for Thomas Cromwell and publicly and very vocally calling for an end to the clergy's right to tithes. This was his undoing. Hauled before Thomas Cranmer, Archbishop of Canterbury, he was flung into jail, where he died in June 1536, lamenting, in a final letter, his fall from grace after a lifetime of achievement. He was, he wrote, 'now by long imprisonment brought to extreme misery, for-saken by his kinsmen, destitute of his friends, comfortless and succourless'.

UNGOVERNABLE

Back in Rastell's home town, an old running sore, the abuse of common lands, had reopened and was beginning to make the city almost ungovernable. The Leet had triggered it in 1522 by ordering that at least half the enclosed common lands should be ploughed and sown, meaning that they would still be under cultivation on Lammas Day, 1 August, the tra-ditional date for opening them up to general use as pasture.

Acts of vandalism in 1524 were followed by serious distur-bances on Lammas Day 1525, when the annual ride by the Chamberlains to open up the common lands was accompa-nied by a large, rowdy crowd, who tore up hedges, battered down fences and even filled in a ditch. Meanwhile, another angry crowd gathered in the streets and as the Chamberlains rode back towards the walls they closed the New Gate, shut-ting them out. At the same time, another group broke into the treasury in St Mary's Hall and seized the box containing rents for the common lands.

Faced with what looked like insurrection, Thomas Grey, 2nd Marquess of Dorset, was ordered by royal commission to regain control of Coventry, with a force of 2,000 men, if need be. In the event, the ringleaders were handed over, a total of thirty-seven rioters were committed to the castles of Warwick and Kenilworth, and a further seven were sent to the Marshalsea prison in London. Five of them were later nailed by the ears to the pillory, back in Coventry.

HUMPHREY REYNOLDS

The next serious threat to the ruling order in Coventry came from an unlikely source, the younger son of a family of fullers in the city. In 1533, Humphrey Reynolds made a special supplication to the king, claiming that as a younger son, he was being disadvantaged from competing for land and property by the weight of financial muscle exercised by wealthy merchants and the monastic orders, particularly the Benedictines. His solution was to propose that urban monasteries such as Coventry's should be left enough money to live on, but that the bulk of their income should be used, instead, to fund a royal military presence in every monastic establishment, with officials and armed men to enforce the law. This force would also be used to govern the city in place of a magistracy that he claimed was incapable of keeping order.

A flagrant challenge to Coventry's hard-won liberties, Reynolds's proposals were stoutly opposed by city officials, but the impression had been given of a greedy monastic order and a city virtually ungovernable. It was a message that may well have helped to encourage what happened next.

DISSOLVING THE MONASTERIES

In late 1534, the membership of the Corpus Christi guild met to consider their future in harsh economic times. Reduced in numbers and unable in some cases to afford even to take office, they decided to merge with the Holy Trinity guild, ending almost two centuries of political, economic and cultural influence in Coventry.

Another sign of the old order beginning to crumble was unusual activity at the commercial centrepiece of the city's calendar, the Coventry Great Fair in June. At one fair in the mid-1530s, it was reported that the Prior of Selby in Yorkshire had sold his cross-staff to the wife of a London goldsmith and that the Cistercian monks of nearby Stoneleigh Abbey had disposed of silver religious artefacts to the value of £14.

Then the blow fell. On 1 October 1538, as Henry VIII's attack on the monasteries gathered pace, the house of the Carmelites, or Whitefriars, was surrendered to the king's commissioners. Four days later it was the turn of the Greyfriars. The friars, fourteen Carmelites and eleven Greyfriars, were summarily turned out without a pension between them, and work began almost immediately to prepare friary buildings for demolition and sale.

On 15 January 1539, the Benedictine prior Thomas Camwell and twelve monks formally surrendered the priory and its huge cathedral church to the king's chief commissioner in the region, Dr John London. The following day he accepted the surrender of the twelve remaining Carthusian monks at the Coventry Charterhouse, and the two great Cistercian abbeys at Coombe and Stoneleigh followed within days. Within three months, the entire edifice of the city's monastic life had been brought crashing to earth.

Coventry's misfortune was to be tied into a diocese with Lichfield, a cathedral run by secular canons instead of monks, a state of affairs very much favoured by the monk-hating Henry. On top of that, successive bishops of Coventry and Lichfield had long made Lichfield the chief focus of their activities, allowing their palace in Coventry to become virtually a ruin, and with two cathedrals in one diocese, it was always going to be hard to protect both.

Nevertheless, Bishop Rowland Lee petitioned Henry's chief minister Thomas Cromwell to save Coventry's cathedral, arguing that uses could be found for it. With the mayor and council adding their own entreaties, it looked for a month or two as if it might be saved. Coventry's priory still ranked ninth in the Benedictine rich list, however, its cathedral church a blaze of gold, and Henry and his advisers were not going to pass up the opportunity to acquire its riches. It was the only cathedral in England to be destroyed at the Dissolution.

AFTERMATH

By July 1539, royal agents were in Coventry to begin pulling down the great cathedral church and the church of the Whitefriars, although it was to prove slow work. Nearly

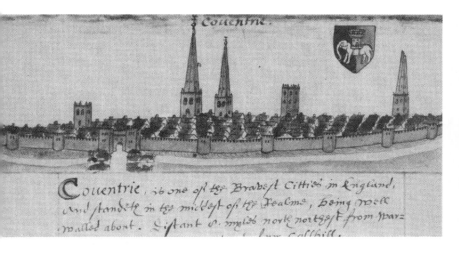

William Smyth's sketch, the earliest surviving image of the city, shows a cathedral tower still standing (centre right). (Image courtesy of Culture Coventry (Coventry Archives))

forty years later, one of the cathedral's towers was still standing, clearly visible in the earliest surviving image of the city,
William Smyth's sketch of 1576.

Other buildings vanished much more quickly. By 1542,
monastic properties belonging to the Greyfriars were being
demolished and huge quantities of stone were already being
removed from the Charterhouse site. Within five years the
Hospital of St John in the Burges had been sold to a royal
civil servant, John Hales. The Holy Trinity guild, once one of
the most powerful in England, had been suppressed and its
chapel, the collegiate church of St John's Bablake, had been
confiscated. The chapel of St George next to Gosford Bridge
went the same way shortly afterwards, and all the guild
and chantry chapels were ripped out of the churches of St
Michael's and Holy Trinity.

The final act of despoliation took place in 1552 when
the wall paintings in these churches were whitewashed and
their tools of worship – chalices, pyxes, censers, proces-
sional crosses, bells, chasubles, satin and gold copes and
gold thread – were loaded onto carts and trundled off to the
royal coffers. In little more than a decade, the physical and
spiritual heart of the city had been ripped out and its economy devastated. For nearly 500 years, the monasteries had
been good for business in Coventry. Now they were gone.

It was left to two wealthy outsiders to provide some small
comfort in Coventry's hour of greatest need. In late 1541 the
merchant and former Lord Mayor of London, Sir William
Holles, who was born at Stoke Hall just outside Coventry,
bequeathed the city £200 to build a new market cross,
replacing a predecessor constructed at Cross Cheaping
in 1422. Modelled on a cross at Abingdon in Berkshire, it
was 57ft high, superbly ornamented with figures of kings,
monks and saints, and became an object of admiration for
travellers writing about the city for the next 200 years.

Another London merchant, Sir Thomas White, who had
no local family connections but had clearly done a lot of

business with Coventry over the years, was even more generous. In 1548 he gave the city the handsome sum of £1,400, with which the council bought property being sold off by the king's commissioners, notably the Trinity guild's headquarters, St Mary's Hall, which was to become the administrative base for the mayor and council.

A FINAL REBELLION

In February 1555, with the fiercely Catholic Mary on the throne, the prominent Protestant cleric Lawrence Saunders, rector of All Hallows in London, was burned at the stake in the hollow in the Cheylesmore Park. Saunders had connections with Coventry. He'd lived in the city as a child for some years and his brother Edward was its fanatically Catholic recorder in 1553. For his prosecutors, however, the real point was to make his martyrdom, cruelly prolonged by the deliberate use of green wood in the fire, a warning to this rebellious, fanatic town.

In September of the same year, Robert Glover from Mancetter in north Warwickshire and a Coventry capper named Cornelius Bungey followed him to the stake. They had been condemned for arguing that a priest had no power to absolve any sinner of his sins. The hollow where they died was levelled early in the nineteenth century, but in 1854, the park keeper, William Mansfield, made a grim discovery while digging in the area:

When I had dug down about six feet from the surface, I came to some very black soil, different from that which I had dug through. I also found some charred or burnt wood, some cinders and pieces of bright coal. I also found a number of bones and a piece of silk, which might have been part of a dress, close by the bones. I had got down to a rock in which was what appeared to be a grave, and the bones and piece of silk were in the grave.

It was a pitiful reminder of the brave men and women who had submitted themselves to unspeakable agonies for their faith, but it did provide an accurate location for the memorial cross that in 1910 was erected close to the spot.

6

WHAT FOOLS YE BE

On Saturday 17 August 1565, the mayor, Edmund Brownell, led a civic party arrayed in their scarlet to the Bishop Gate in the town wall, where they awaited the arrival of Queen Elizabeth I on royal progress. It was the queen's first visit to Coventry. She stayed for two days, took in special performances of the mystery plays and was presented with the obligatory £100 in gold, at which she exclaimed, 'It is a good gift of gold. I have few such gifts.'

John Throckmorton, recorder of Coventry, delivered a welcome speech of toe-curling sycophancy, in which he heaped lavish praise on the queen's father, skirting carefully around the damage that Henry VIII had inflicted on the city in his pursuit of the monasteries. It was to be Elizabeth's only visit to Coventry, yet the feeling locally was that she had a soft spot for the place. In addressing a large crowd from an oriel window at Whitefriars, where she was staying, it was reputed that she had admonished them with a fond, 'Ah, men of Coventry. What fools ye be!' when the flattery became a little cloying.

The council insisted on sending the queen some of their more thorny disputes to adjudicate, and while there is no evidence that she even got to see these complaints, in 1568 she did give Coventry the sole right to manufacture some new kinds of cloth, formerly imported from Amsterdam

– utterfynes and crompstyles. Within two years there was a Dutch chapel in the city, used by the specialist weavers brought in to teach locals the mysteries of this new manu-facturing. They brought with them a modest recovery in the economy too.

JOHN HALES

If Recorder Throckmorton's welcome speech had reeked of excessive deference towards the queen, it positively dripped with venom towards the man with whom, embarrassingly, she was staying: John Hales, her father's former Clerk to the Hanaper. In the chaos that followed the Dissolution, Hales had acquired Whitefriars, re-named Hales Place, along with much of the Benedictine Priory site and the Hospital of St John in the Burges, by virtue of his position as a royal civil servant, and he was hated for it. The council's chief complaint against him now was that he had agreed with Henry VIII to found a free grammar school in the king's name and then had reneged on his promise to fund it, using 'sinister, under-hand and unjust means' to do so. Ironically, the new school, housed in the Hospital of St John, had been Elizabeth's first stop as she entered the city, allowing her time to make a small gift of money to its library, and she clearly thought the accusations sufficiently serious to have them investigated, although no evidence of wrong-doing was found.

The campaign against Hales in Coventry, which lasted until his death in 1572, may have been a little unfair on him. All the evidence suggests that he was fond of Coventry and tried in his years of power and influence to support the city where he could. A cultured man, with several pamphlets on education and administration to his credit, he had already faced the queen's fury, and been briefly imprisoned, after writing a tract on the toxic issue of the succession to the throne if Elizabeth should fail to have children. Some years after his death, Hales Place became one of the secret printing centres for the anonymous Martin Marprelate tracts, which attacked the bishops of the Anglican Church.

RISE OF THE PURITANS

That Coventry should be one of the nerve centres of anti-clericalism is not, perhaps, surprising. In 1555, the year that the Protestant martyr Saunders went to the stake in the hollow in Cheylesmore Park, one of the city's sheriffs, Richard Hopkins, was 'put out for religion' and thrown into the Fleet prison in London. Hopkins, it was alleged, had been ordered to torture Saunders and had refused to do so. On his release, he gathered up his wife and eight children and fled to Basel in what is now Switzerland, where, as a Protestant, he felt safer.

The death of Queen Mary had doused the fires, but as the Protestant ascendancy that followed took a grip on the city, Coventry found its old ways increasingly being challenged. A new Puritanism, advocated by clergy and prominent citizens, found its voice in a Leet Book entry from 1547, which stated:

> Those that be of the poorest sort do sit all day in the alehouse drinking and playing cards at tables and spend all they get prodigally on them-selves, to the high displeasure of God. Whereas, if it were spent at home in their own houses, their wives and children would get a part of it.

In 1549, 'good ministers' had been sent to Coventry to sort this out, and the mayor and aldermen decreed that there would be a levy on every household to pay for it. Before long, images and relics from city churches were being destroyed and their colourful wall paintings whitewashed. The registers of St Michael's Church were burned as they were thought to contain 'some marks of Popery', and Puritan supporters even set out to tear down Coventry's new and highly decorative market cross, paid for in a generous bequest by locally-born

merchant and former Lord Mayor of London, Sir William
Holles. Only a large crowd of butchers, armed with cleavers,
gave them second thoughts.

The new cross, admired by travellers writing about Coventry for
the next 200 years. (Image courtesy of Culture Coventry (Coventry
Archives))

In 1561, the 'good ministers' had moved against the city's celebrated Hock Tuesday play, which took the defeat of the Danes in 1002 as its theme and had been performed for at least 150 years. The play had become a symbol of civic pride and there was outrage when it was suppressed, but that was only the beginning.

COVENTRY'S MYSTERY PLAYS

The first reference to a pageant house – for storing the wagons, or pageants, on which the plays were staged – comes from 1392, but it is probable that the plays were in existence at least forty years before. There were ten of them in all, covering the story of the world from Creation to Domesday, each a source of pride to the craft company, or guild, that created it. Other cities like York and Chester boasted an impressive register of plays themselves, but none enjoyed a greater level of royal patronage.

Henrys V, VI, VII and VIII all made special visits to see the plays. Richard III was a spectator in the summer of 1485, months before his defeat at Bosworth. Henry VIII's daughter Mary saw a special performance of the Mercers play, depicting the later life of the Virgin Mary, in 1526, while her sister Elizabeth witnessed four plays during her 1565 visit, surrounded by her entourage and respectful citizens at a 'station', or place of performance, in Earl Street. By then, however, the writing was on the wall for this famous Coventry tradition. Despite a desperate rear-guard action fought by traditionalists like master upholsterer Thomas Massey, the last complete cycle of the plays was performed in 1579. Only one has survived the rollercoaster of history in any substantive form: the Shearmen and Tailors' Nativity play, with its ranting Herod and its blend of earthy humour and raw emotion.

MARY, QUEEN OF SCOTS

Queen Elizabeth may have only visited Coventry once, but in November 1569 it was to the city that she turned when rebellion broke out among the Catholic earls in the north. She needed to move the focus of their revolt, her cousin and prisoner, Mary, Queen of Scots, from Tutbury Castle in Staffordshire to a more secure confinement further south, and perhaps Coventry's loud and repeated protestations of undying loyalty influenced her choice.

The letter that she sent to the mayor survives, and is a model of brevity and directness. The good people of Coventry were, she wrote, to ensure the Scottish queen was 'safely kept and guarded', and were to obey her jailers' instructions to the letter.

Mary was moved to Coventry on 25 November and was lodged initially at the Bull Inn on Smithford Street, originally the home of the powerful Onley family and the place where Henry VII had lodged just two days after his victory at Bosworth Field. Her chief jailer, the Earl of Shrewsbury, expressed his nervousness at the lack of security, despite having 400 soldiers with him and the gates on the walls being double-manned. She was therefore moved to St Mary's Hall, a better protected but miserably cramped confinement for a queen who brought a sizeable retinue of Scottish and French retainers with her.

There, in a story that has 'apocryphal' written all over it, it is said that Mary's jailers positioned a portrait of Elizabeth in front of a low and narrow doorway, through which the 6ft-tall Scottish queen would have to bow as she entered. Mary, the tale went, simply turned her back and reversed through the doorway, thereby delivering one of the Elizabethan age's rudest insults to her captor. Whatever the truth of it, Elizabeth's trust in her 'fools' in Coventry must have frightened the life out of them, and they were no doubt thoroughly

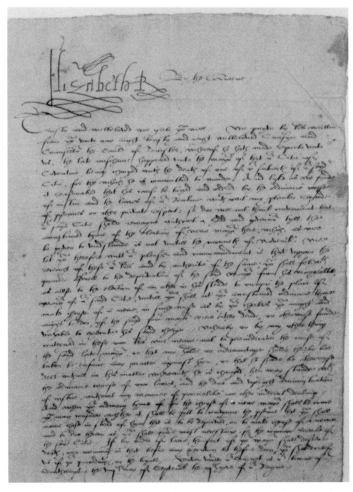

Elizabeth's letter to the people of Coventry, warning them to take good care of Mary. (Image courtesy of Culture Coventry (Coventry Archives))

relieved when, early in the new year, Mary was moved back to Tutbury.

UPSETTING THE MAYOR

The authorities' displeasure with 'Papist' pastimes did not
end with their suppression of the mystery plays. Coventry's
festive processions, a colourful feature of the city's life that
had been a major visitor attraction for nigh-on 200 years,
were banned from the 1560s. The city's 10ft-high maypole,
the centrepiece of many a summer celebration, was taken
down in 1591, not to be seen again until the Restoration
nearly seventy years later. From 1595, anybody caught playing football in the street could be taken to the common jail
and kept there for as long as the mayor chose.

An order from 1588 had decreed that opening shops, playing games and even idly walking around on a Sunday were
not permitted, and that was followed up with further bans
on the playing of indoor games and even sitting around in the
streets. Dissent was not tolerated. In November 1592, John
Boothe, a glover, was arrested for being a 'very babbling,
disordered person', especially against the mayor and other
important citizens. He was thrown into jail but released after
making an abject apology.

In such a highly charged atmosphere, with the city's economy still fragile, suspicions that immigrants were taking
jobs from locals predictably began to surface. Strangers
who were unemployed and unable to support themselves
had to leave the city, and this was followed up, in 1598,
by an order that a stranger who had married a Coventry
woman had to take her to his birthplace for a year before
being allowed to settle in the city.

Intolerance towards outsiders could easily extend to
invited visitors too. In 1600, actors from the visiting Lord
Chandos's Men, performing at the Angel Inn on Smithford
Street, were arrested for contempt against 'master may-
or's pleasure' and were not released from jail until they
had made a full apology. On that occasion, William
Shakespeare, rising star of London's theatrical firmament,

was not amongst the travelling players, but the evidence suggests that he had trodden the boards in Coventry with at least two other acting companies in the 1590s, learning the lesson, no doubt, that as a writer, powerful interests were not to be trifled with.

What Lord Chandos's men had done to upset the mayor wasn't recorded, but if the authorities were looking for an excuse for what appeared to be paranoid and overbearing behaviour, they could have pointed to the events of November 1605.

THE GUNPOWDER PLOT

Against expectations, Elizabeth I's successor, James I, had not tempered her harsh policies towards Catholics, and in early 1605, Warwickshire landowner Robert Catesby, whose principal estate was at Lapworth, decided the time had come to hit back. At 32, the charismatic Catesby came from a noted Catholic family. His father had been imprisoned for harbouring a priest and he himself had failed to complete his university degree because he refused to sign the obligatory Protestant Oath of Supremacy.

The Catesbys had a history in Coventry. William de Catesby had risen from Warwickshire peasant roots to become a knight in 1339, and had later purchased a substantial house and up to forty tenements in the town. For nearly 150 years his descendants had been among Coventry's most powerful landlords, with property in Bishop Street, West Orchard and Earl Street, but perhaps surprisingly had never sought public office, the traditional route to power and influence. There had been a Catesby Lane in Coventry, but it does not appear on John Speed's map of 1610. It had been written out of history, possibly by an earlier Catesby's ill-advised support for Richard III at the Battle of Bosworth, for which he had been executed, or by the events of 1605.

Robert Catesby (second right), chief conspirator and man with Coventry connections. (The History Press)

Robert Catesby's plan was to blow up the king, the Commons and the Lords, using gunpowder stashed in cellars below the Westminster chamber where they met for the State Opening of Parliament. Then he would place James I's eldest daughter, Elizabeth, on the throne and marry her to a prominent Catholic to seal the succession.

Elizabeth, then aged 9, was living at Coombe Abbey under the care and protection of Sir John Harrington and his wife, old friends to whom James had entrusted her education. Now, she was to be the unwitting instrument of rebellion.

Catesby gathered together a group of conspirators that included, as well as former soldier Guy Fawkes, several more Warwickshire gentlemen: his cousins, Thomas and Robert Winter, and John Grant, who owned a manor house near Stratford. Fearing that Catholic Lords and MPs would be killed by the explosion too, they decided to warn a number of them to stay away on the date of the State Opening, 5 November. That was a fatal mistake. The government was tipped off and arrested Guy Fawkes on 4 November as he guarded the thirty-six barrels of gunpowder. Catesby and his fellow plotters fled back to the Midlands, hoping to seize the young princess, but they were too late.

Word of the plot had reached Coombe, and on the same day Elizabeth was moved into Coventry and lodged at Palace Yard, the substantial mansion owned by the staunchly Protestant Hopkins family in Earl Street. The Gunpowder Plot ended with a siege at Holbeche House in Staffordshire. There, Catesby and several other plotters were killed, and awaiting those who survived was a string of grisly executions in London the following January. But might there have been a different outcome?

On the night of 4 November, no more than a couple of hundred yards from Palace Yard, Robert Winter and another of the plotters, Stephen Littleton, were staying at the Bull Inn on Smithford Street, before heading out to the plotters' rendezvous at Dunchurch the following day. Had they known Princess Elizabeth was so close, an opportunity might have presented itself to spirit her away from her escort, who presumably had relaxed, believing that they were secure in the heart of Protestant Coventry.

A TASTE FOR CULTURE?

In the midst of all this Catholic rebellion and priggish Puritanism, a modest flowering of culture was taking root in Coventry. In 1601, John Tovey, headmaster of King Henry VIII School, appealed for books to supplement his scholars' meagre supply, and before long there was an annual stipend of 13s 4d from the will of the merchant William Wheate for someone to look after them. The library would in time become sadly neglected – by the 1830s it was found that some of its volumes, largely religious works, had been used to light fires – but from the start it was open to scholars of the city, not just the school, ensuring that Coventry, alongside Norwich, has a claim to being the home of the first public library in England.

PHILEMON HOLLAND

The embodiment of this new strain of intellectualism was undoubtedly Philemon Holland: doctor, teacher and the greatest classical translator of his age, who had made his home in the city since the 1590s. Holland, whose translations of the work of classical authors like Pliny, Plutarch and Suetonius are still held in high regard, worked initially as a doctor, ministering to the poor, but taught at the grammar school from 1608 and became its headmaster twenty years later. He died in 1637, aged 85, and his tomb, with the punning epitaph that he composed, can still be seen in Holy Trinity Church.

Holy Trinity also featured in the life of one of Holland's most remarkable pupils, James Illedge, who was born blind to a poor family in the city, yet overcame what was then an almost insurmountable disadvantage to become a lecturer or preacher at Holy Trinity and later vicar of Ansty and Shilton, until his death in 1644.

JAMES I

It was Philemon Holland, dubbed Translator General in England, who was chosen to give the welcome oration to James I when he visited the city on 2 September 1617. At a huge banquet in St Mary's Hall, the king was given a gold cup, valued at more than £200. James was suitably gracious, promising that wherever he went he would drink out of his Coventry cup, but in truth he had his suspicions of the Puritans of Coventry and was always wary of them. In 1611 he had commanded that they should kneel while receiving the Holy Sacrament, something that many of them found hard to stomach, and in 1621 he demanded assurances from the Bishop of Coventry and Lichfield that they were obeying the rules of the Church before he would grant the city a new charter of governance.

THE GOVERNING CHARTER

Granted by royal assent on 18 July 1621, the charter established two new three-day fairs in the city in April and August, set up a 'Court of Orphans' to adjudicate on the city's care of bereaved children, and established the 'Close Corporation' that was to rule Coventry, making it at times, sadly, a byword for civic corruption, until the municipal reform legislation of 1835.

The Governing Charter, so called because the corporation later decided that it superseded all other charters, either before or after, instituted a new system of government, with the mayor and ten aldermen (one for each ward) sitting with a 'Grand Council' of up to twenty more councillors. They were self-selecting and their appointment would be for life. A second 'Common Council' of twenty-five was nominated by the mayor and aldermen, but was only convened when the Grand Council wanted a second opinion – and that was pretty rare.

COVENTRY VERSUS WARWICKSHIRE

The new way of doing things owed much to Coventry's able and well-connected town clerk, Humphrey Repton, who codified Coventry's liberties as an independent and equal-ranking county to Warwickshire. The city's relationship with the county that surrounded it had always been distant at best. The merchant oligarchy that ruled Coventry kept themselves aloof from the landed gentry who governed Warwickshire, while they in turn made Warwick, not Coventry, the focus of their interest and patronage. They borrowed money from Coventry's merchants but did not marry their daughters. They frequented the city's markets but not its social circles. The divide between these two power cliques deepened dramatically in 1635, when the imperious Charles I ill-advisedly decided to raise revenues for foreign military adventures by imposing on his subjects a tax known as 'Ship Money', reflecting the king's ambitions for his navy.

When news of Charles's high-handed tax plans broke, Coventry pleaded poverty, citing the slow recovery of its economy since the depths of recession in the 1550s, but what really riled the men who ruled the city was that Ship Money would be administered by the Sheriff of Warwickshire, who would decide what share of the county's burden would fall on Coventry. When he assessed it as one-eighth (£500 out of £4,000) there was uproar, and direct appeal was made to the Privy Council, demonstrating Coventry's well-practised ability to find routes into government at the highest level. In the event, it had to find something like £200, but even then it shunned Warwickshire, paying what it owed directly to the king's treasury.

THE CITY'S FORTUNES

While the production of cloth, in many different forms, still represented the core of Coventry's economy, new ways of earning its living were beginning to emerge. In 1627, a silk weavers' company was established in the city, indicating that a number of craftsmen had been at work in this field for some time. Within 100 years, silk weaving would become a staple industry.

Just north of the city, the old craft of mining coal from shallow reserves was beginning to turn into an industry, and in 1622, Matthew Collins, a Coventry merchant, and John Potter, whose line of work was almost certainly in mining, obtained a licence to extract coal on the Griff estate, owned by Sir Thomas Beaumont. Despite the fierce, and at times violent, opposition of miners already working in neighbouring Bedworth, they were soon making handsome profits from a trade that in time would make Coventry an access point for a much wider market.

Even though its time as the Midlands' most important city was beginning to run out, Coventry was still being described as 'a great thoroughfare town', standing at the crossroads of England at the heart of the country's north–south trading web. And despite its somewhat reduced circumstances, visitors to the city could still be favourably impressed by its air of imposing antiquity. A Lieutenant Hammond from East Anglia, passing through in 1634, praised its many fair streets and buildings and its market cross, but was most struck by St Mary's Hall – a building, he observed, 'with a stately ascending entrance, the upper end adorned with rich hangings and all about with fayre pictures, one more especially of a noble lady, whose memory they have cause not to forget'.

TROUBLE AHEAD

Godiva's legendary support for the put-upon townsfolk had indeed not been forgotten as tensions still flared around that perennial flashpoint, the abuse of common lands. On Lammas Day in 1639, an angry crowd had marched out to spoil a field of oats and throw down a wall erected on common land. Five ringleaders were arrested and thrown into jail, but that night more than 300 supporters, armed with clubs and iron bars, gathered outside, intent on battering their way in, and the men were hurriedly released.

As the relationship between King and Parliament descended towards civil war, it became apparent to more far-seeing Coventrians that their city's central location and its renowned defensive wall would make it a prized possession in any conflict to come. In December 1641, the council ordered the purchase of new cannons, having found the existing weapons defective in hastily-arranged trials. Alongside a significant stockpiling of arms and ammunition, most of it in St Mary's Hall, the council also ordered that every householder 'of abilitie' was to provide at least one musket, 'so that this citie maie have in readiness upon any sudden occasion at least 500 muskets for its defence and safeguard'. Within months, those defences would be put to the test.

7

A GREAT REBELLION

On 13 August 1642, a royal herald appeared at the gates of Coventry, bearing news that King Charles I was approaching and wished to enter. The king had with him a small force of 800 cavalry and 300 foot soldiers, but the response from inside the walls was that he was welcome, but only with an escort of 200 men. Charles flew into a rage and ordered the herald, Sir William Dugdale, Warwickshire country gentleman and former pupil of Coventry's King Henry VIII School, to declare the mayor, aldermen and indeed the whole city, traitors to the Crown.

Coventry's defiance would not have surprised Charles. Like his father, he was suspicious of the city and expected no less. Yet it was also a place whose central location and highly defensible town wall made it an ideal military headquarters from which to launch his war with Parliament.

QUIET STRUGGLE

For months, that coming conflict had manifested itself in a quiet but ferocious struggle for supremacy inside the city itself between the king's party, led by aldermen Henry Million and John Clarke, and those who supported Parliament, led by their fellow aldermen, John Barker and Thomas Basnett.

In June, John Barker had defied the Earl of Northampton, Recorder of the city, when he had tried to impose the king's Commission of Array, Charles's attempt to raise troops around the country.

Tensions were turned up a further notch on 10 August, when Million and Clarke, on the instructions of Northampton, tried to seize the county magazine, stored in the tower of Spon Gate. They were ousted by a force led by Barker and Basnett, who now declared that Coventry was held for Parliament, forcing Northampton himself to make an undignified exit from the city.

UNDER SIEGE

All of this Charles now knew as he contemplated the city's defiance from a slight rise to the south, known as Park Hill. Declaring that he would 'lay the city in a heap of rubbish, ere he left it', he ordered his artillery to open fire, and on 19 August the siege of Coventry began. It lasted two days, and accounts of it differ wildly. In one, the royal gunners inflicted little damage, barring a stray shot that hit Whitefriars and killed the bedridden Lady Hales and one of her servants. The other version was that a breach in the walls was made, but that the royal forces were confronted by citizens, pouring out in fighting array, and suffered severe casualties in the battle that followed. Whatever the truth, Charles and his army began to withdraw as news came through that Lord Brooke, Parliament's most important supporter in Warwickshire, and General John Hampden were approaching from the south with eleven troops of horse and 4,800 foot soldiers.

Whether it liked it or not, and within the city support for the king and his enemies was fairly evenly split, Coventry was now a parliamentary bastion. John Barker was made governor, a garrison was installed and steps

were taken to boost the city's already impressive defences.
A stone wall dividing the Great Park and the Little Park,
which had hidden the king's gunners as they bombarded
Coventry, was torn down. Houses that had crept out along
every main road beyond the town wall were demolished
to improve the field of fire. Apart from New Gate, Spon
Gate, Bishop Gate and Gosford Gate, all the gates in the
wall were blocked up and cannons were mounted at each
of those remaining open.

It worked. Over the next two years, while Leicester, and
notably Birmingham, suffered from repeated pillaging as the
war swung across the Midlands, Coventry and its garrison
appeared too strong a nut to crack, even for such a talented
and bull-headed Royalist commander as Prince Rupert, the
king's nephew.

SOBER COMPANY

Coventry had become a refuge for many who might face
persecution from the king's forces, and among those seeking
shelter in the city were more than thirty Puritan ministers,
led by the eminent preacher and theologian Richard Baxter.
He clearly felt at home in Coventry, among this 'sober,
wise and religious company', and his companions included
two men who would go on to become much-loved and
influential ministers in the city. Obadiah Grew, formerly
headmaster of the grammar school at Atherstone in north
Warwickshire, became vicar of St Michael's in 1644, and
in the same year John Bryan, a protégé of Lord Brooke,
accepted the living of Holy Trinity.

When Baxter announced in 1645 that he was joining
the New Model Army as a regimental chaplain, frantic,
but unsuccessful, efforts were made to get him to change
his mind, as he had been a moderating influence on the
increasingly fraught relationship between the townsfolk,

the parliamentary garrison that protected them, and armies passing through.

In the winter of 1643 there had been fighting between the garrison and troops from the Earl of Denbigh's army, and in 1646 a parliamentary army that had been fighting in Scotland was refused entry to the city, bivouacking instead on Gosford Green, from where they sent in to Coventry for provisions.

SENT TO COVENTRY

There has been more than one theory put forward for the origin of this expression, meaning to be cold-shouldered, or shunned. Possibly its origins lay with the Carthusian order's practice of sending recalcitrant monks to be 'sorted out' at its Coventry Charterhouse, or perhaps it was a legacy of the city's unenviable reputation in the fifteenth century as a place where powerful wrongdoers sentenced to death in London could be sent for execution.

It is much more likely, however, that the phrase came from the aftermath of a single event during the Second Civil War, the defeat of the Royalist Duke of Hamilton's Scottish army at Preston in 1648. Prisoners were sent in large numbers to Coventry and were lodged in the Leather Hall in West Orchard, the towers of Spon and Greyfriars gates and the bridewell, or house of correction, that had been established behind Bablake Church in 1571.

Their alien Scottishness and Royalist sympathies, as well as the extra pressure they must have put on the city's food supplies at a time of poor harvests, undoubtedly caused resentment among locals whose attitude towards them would certainly have been extremely hostile. The expression was first used in *The History of the Great Rebellion*, written by the prominent Royalist Edward Hyde, first Earl of Clarendon, in the 1670s, and published in 1702.

Greyfriars Gate from the south, drawn by Nathaniel Troughton in the early nineteenth century. (Image courtesy of Culture Coventry (Coventry Archives))

ROBERT BEAKE

A major in the parliamentary army, Beake was a draper by trade and in 1651 became one of Coventry's sheriffs, an office that was often a precursor to greater things. Three years later he was elected as one of two MPs for Coventry and Warwickshire, and the following year became mayor of the city.

Robert Beake's mayoral legacy rests largely on the diary he kept during his year of office, which survives as a quirky and telling picture of life in a provincial city under Cromwell's protectorate. It is a daily account of his doings as mayor and chief magistrate, his Puritan zeal tempered by a gruff humanity. Beake was a stickler for rules and an ardent supporter of Sabbatarianism – the idea that Sunday was purely for religion and quiet contemplation – yet to dismiss him as merely an officious and interfering busybody, out to stop everybody else having fun, is to miss the essence of the man.

As mayor, Beake was responsible for ensuring that the city's streets were kept in good order, that its tradesmen obeyed rules on prices and quality and that those who looked after the vulnerable and needy fulfilled their duties. He accomplished all of this, and more, with a commendable incorruptibility, refusing gifts that were clearly meant to influence him. In his diary for 19 November 1655, the mayor expressed his regret at having to place three Quakers in a cage for travelling on the Lord's Day: 'It grieved me that this poor deluded people should undergo punishment of such a nature.' He released one Goody Pywell from jail because her legs had swollen, attempted conciliation between neighbours who had come to blows, and intervened to prevent stocks of corn being hoarded to force up the price.

Beake's steadfastness as a supporter of the protectorate won him the post of Admiralty Commissioner, and once his mayoral year was over, the focus of his activities moved to London. After the death of Cromwell and the end of the Commonwealth, however, he was back in Coventry, ready to make a decisive intervention in events. Conflict within the army had led to fears that the city might become the headquarters for the radical Major-General John Lambert, and in September 1659, the mayor, Richard Hicks, ordered the magazine in St Mary's Hall to be opened and arms distributed.

More than 150 men, commanded by Major Beake, gathered in St Michael's churchyard and marched on a detachment of soldiers helping to guard the city, demanding in the name of Parliament that that responsibility should be handed over to them. Their success – when challenged the troops simply marched away – showed that Coventry now aligned itself with those who saw the return of the monarchy as inevitable.

THE RESTORATION

As a hotbed of opposition to Charles I, Coventry realised that it had much to do to placate his son, Charles II. On the day of his coronation, St George's Day 1661, there were bonfires and feasts in the streets and it was reported that the conduits ran with claret wine, paid for by wealthy alderman Thomas Norton. The city sent a delegation to welcome the new king, bearing lavish gifts, including silver plate worth £160. It acquired new portraits of both Charles I and Charles II, and painted the royal coat of arms on freshly whitewashed walls in St Mary's Hall.

It was all too late, however. In November 1661, rumours of plots against Charles II surfaced and Coventry was implicated – wrongly, as it turned out. A force was dispatched to the city and its commander, Sir Henry Jones, demanded the keys to the city gates. Along with other parliamentary strongholds like Gloucester and Northampton, Coventry was about to pay for its 'great rebellion'.

COVENTRY'S TOWN WALL

An alarming outbreak of lawlessness, with organised gangs of criminals roaming the countryside, may have been the spur in 1329 for Coventry's prosperous ruling class to seek royal consent to build a wall. Yet, curiously, it took another twenty-five years for work on it to begin, and progress was rarely more than sporadic over the next century and a half. By the 1530s it was edging towards completion, just in time for the city to experience the devastation wrought on its economy and heritage by Henry VIII's commissioners. However, the town wall had protected Coventry from the worst ravages of the Wars of the Roses, and its majestic red sandstone had become one of the sights of provincial England, commented

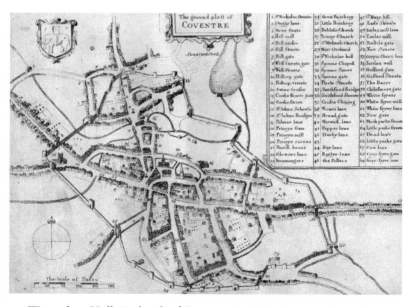

Wenceslaus Hollar's sketch of Coventry in 1656, showing the wall still standing. (Image courtesy of Culture Coventry (Coventry Archives))

on by many travellers. Writing in 1639, on the eve of the
Civil War, John Taylor the Water Poet offered an enthusiastic
first impression of Coventry. It was, he wrote, 'a fair, famous,
sweet and ancient city so walled about with such strength
and neatnesse as no city in England may compare with it'.

In the summer of 1662, the king ordered the Earl of
Northampton, his Lord Lieutenant in Warwickshire and the
son of the man who had fled the city in such haste twenty
years before, to 'slight' the walls. Northampton arrived on
22 July with a large body of Warwickshire gentry and soldiers, and in three weeks tore down large sections of it, while
enjoying liberal hospitality from the council in the shape
of at least one huge banquet in St Mary's Hall and copious
quantities of alcohol, delivered nightly to their lodgings. In a
gesture clearly born out of revenge, Northampton declared
that stone from the wall, that ultimate symbol of civic pride,
should be used to help poor men in Coventry build better
homes for themselves, at just 12*d* per cartload.

THE KING'S SPY

The destruction of the town wall represented interference in
Coventry's affairs by the Crown in a way that would have
been unthinkable before the Civil War, but it was just the
beginning. Clerics Obadiah Grew and John Bryan were
ejected from their livings, while prominent supporters of
Parliament like Robert Beake and John Barker resigned
before they could be sacked.

The Corporation Act of 1661 and the Act of Uniformity
that followed it a year later were designed to root out non-conformists in local government and the clergy. Yet remarkably,
Dissenters, as they were called, remained strong in the city and
by 1670 had actually come to dominate the council. It was
on their activities that the king's domestic intelligence network
employed Coventry baker Ralph Hope to keep watch as a

'correspondent' or spy. Between 1666 and 1672, Hope wrote many letters, of which fifty-one survive, to Joseph Williamson, Charles's under-secretary of state, reporting on local events and the men who were shaping them.

His first letters concerned the city's economy and in particular the huge sums lost by Coventry clothiers as stocks in warehouses were consumed by the Great Fire of London. He reported on the townsfolk's visceral hatred for Sir Robert Townsend, who had been rewarded for his loyalty to the Royalist cause by being given a lease to Cheylesmore Manor, a gift to Charles from the city that the monarch had been expected to hand back. He identified Dissenters whose politics he believed were unreliable, notably the two sheriffs, Hugh Capel and Francis Cater, both Presbyterians and in his view 'very zealous'. He commented on the influence still wielded by the former minister John Bryan and on non-conformist meetings that were on the rise in the city. They were preaching 'helter skelter' at the Leather Hall, he reported, and the magistrates were not doing enough to suppress them.

Hope's view of his home city was fond but somewhat pessimistic. 'Our cities [sic] reputation be in its wane,' he wrote. 'We are willing to support its ancient, though now dwindling, grandeur as long as we are able.'

And he wasn't above recording portents that spoke ill of the future – a pear tree in full bloom in January, a cloud of flies that darkened the skies, a woman who vomited up pebbles, knives, scissors, glass and bullets.

Yet as he slipped back into obscurity in the early 1670s, there were signs that Coventry's ability to conjure a recovery from dark times had not deserted it.

ROAD TO RECOVERY

In 1658 a new stagecoach service had been established between London and Holyhead in north Wales, passing through the city and improving connections to the capital. Ten years later, in a modest reinstatement of civic pride, Coventry's market cross, a feature of the city that had astonished travellers for more than 150 years, was repaired and re-gilded.

Silk weavers had been working in Coventry for at least sixty years, and alongside the manufacture of new types of cloth, notably 'tammies' (striped and glazed worsteds), the foundations were being laid for what would in the century ahead become one of the city's staple industries: ribbon-making.

The glimmerings of another new industry could be seen, too, in the work of a Coventry craftsman named Samuel Watson, who in 1682 decided to make a clock for Charles II. The king died before it could be delivered, but Watson went on to make an extraordinary astronomical clock for his successor, Queen Anne, that can still be seen in the royal collections at Windsor Castle. On the strength of that, Watson, who had held the office of sheriff of Coventry in 1686, moved to London and quickly became one of the most celebrated clockmakers of the age. Before long, back in his home city, his example would inspire others to hone their skills in making clocks and watches.

HEROES AND VILLAINS

In 1678, in an attempt to recover some of Coventry's once-legendary ability to attract big-spending crowds, the council devised a new procession to accompany the opening of the Great Fair, and gave it a new star – Lady Godiva. For centuries, St George the dragon-slayer had been the key figure in city processions, his mythical associations with the city even giving him a local birthplace, Caludon Castle. Now, Coventry's founding mother, as under-dressed as nature intended, it was whispered, would draw the crowds, with music provided by the city waits, who had been disbanded more than forty years earlier for 'being troublesome'. The first of these new Godivas was not a woman, as it happened, but a boy, the young son of one James Swinnerton – and he was fully dressed. There were limits to titillation in seventeenth-century Coventry.

If the idea of using Godiva was a popular one, then the welcome for it among the citizens could not have matched the enthusiasm with which they greeted James, Duke of Monmouth, Protestant hero and illegitimate son of Charles II, when he visited the city on 18 September 1682. Hundreds of well-wishers greeted him at the city gates, as bells pealed and bonfires were lit in the streets. He spent a night at the Star Inn in Earl Street, carousing with veterans of the parliamentary cause, before making a formal morning call on the mayor, Richard Heyward, who had carefully ignored his visit by failing to welcome him the night before.

The public reaction to Monmouth highlighted Coventry's instinctive support for opponents of the Stuart kings, and the following year the city was accused of being one of the crucibles of the Rye House plot, an alleged conspiracy to assassinate Charles II and his brother James, then Duke of York, as they returned from the races at Newmarket. There is little evidence for Coventry's involvement, or even for the plot itself, but that old Puritan Robert Beake was among those who had his house searched and poor Obadiah Grew, now elderly and blind, spent six months in prison on suspicion of being part of it.

Coventry was punished by being forced to surrender its governing charter. The replacement, dated 10 October 1683, gave the Crown the right to remove and appoint corporation officials and aldermen – interference of the most direct kind. To add injury to insult, the charter cost the city £200.

JAMES AND WILLIAM

In 1684, nearly 200 Coventry non-conformists, or Dissenters, were indicted for failing to attend church and imprisoned for attending conventicles, or assembly meetings, instead. Despite the heavy hand of suppression, however, they were proving a tough nut to crack, and by the turn of the century it was estimated that almost a quarter of all households in the city contained at least one Dissenter. Most were Presbyterians and they were particularly strong among the ranks of the mercers, weavers and clothiers companies.

Oddly enough, it was to these die-hard opponents that the Catholic King James II was most anxious to appeal when he came to Coventry on 1 September 1687. Rightly fearing for his throne, James had earlier that year issued a Declaration of Indulgence that lifted many of the penalties and restrictions on those who did not want to worship the Anglican way. Now, he opted to stay at Palace Yard, home of one of the leaders of the Dissenters in Coventry, Richard Hopkins, and later made the astonishing decision to remove eight city officials and replace them with Dissenters. For his visit, the city produced its customary gift of a gold cup worth more than £200, although the atmosphere soured somewhat when the king promptly turned and gave it to his Master of Horse, Lord Dartmouth, whose father had been imprisoned in Coventry during the Civil War. The embarrassment was compounded at a lavish banquet in St Mary's Hall, when a table groaning with food collapsed, showering the royal guest with what one observer noted was a local speciality called Coventry Custard.

Within little more than a year, James had been deposed by his Protestant son-in-law William of Orange and Coventry found itself dealing with a regime much more to its taste. In early 1690, a newly recruited regiment of foot, commanded by the Earl of Kingston, spent three months in the city, before joining William's campaign in Ireland. Then on 5 June, William himself passed through on his way to his crushing victory over James's forces at the Battle of the Boyne. He was given an effusive welcome in the city, but he did not receive the customary gold cup. After James's graceless insult in giving his away to a subordinate, Coventry no longer did expensive presents for sovereigns.

STINK OF CORRUPTION

As far back as the 1590s, concerns had been raised about the council's mismanagement of income-rich city charities, and in 1641 it had been forced to make good sums of money missing from the accounts of Sir Thomas White's charity. The bitter divisions of the war years, combined with the almost hermetically-sealed nature of the 'Close Corporation' that ran the city, created a climate where naked self-interest and corruption flourished. In 1695 its stench finally reached the Court of Chancery, where the council was accused once more of embezzling sums from Sir Thomas White's charity, the first of a series of cases which over the next twenty-five years resulted in it having to pay back the huge sum of £2,241.

The revenues had been used to line comfortable pockets instead of being spent on the worthy recipients of charity, but it wasn't just financial chicanery with which Coventry was being saddled. The city was already headed down a road that would make it a byword for electoral fraud and municipal corruption in the century to come. The first of many electoral disputes had to be sorted out by the Court of King's Bench in May 1697, when it ruled that Edward Owen had been rightfully chosen as mayor the previous year. Owen, a feltmaker, was the candidate of the Dissenters, but he had a rival, the butcher John Barrett, who was favoured by aldermen of a Tory persuasion. After a protracted war of words, parallel mayor-making ceremonies had been staged for both men, and there was even a struggle in the street between their supporters over Coventry's ceremonial sword and mace.

Eight years later, novelist, journalist and spy Daniel Defoe took a highly jaundiced view of the city's politics in his magisterial work of travel writing, *Tour Through the Whole Island of Great Britain*: 'The mob of Coventry, having at the last election beaten the magistrates, wounded the mayor, disarmed the watchmen and taken away their halberds, so carried on the most violent tumult that has been seen in this nation for many years.'

THE DAVENPORTS

In the religious and political turmoil of the seventeenth century, few families can have experienced such divided loyalties as the wealthy and influential Davenports of Coventry. Born in the 1590s, John and Christopher Davenport were within a year of being the same age, despite being uncle and nephew, and spent their schooldays together at King Henry VIII School. In 1613 both went up to Merton College, Oxford, transferring to Magdalen Hall together the following year. It was at Oxford that their lives headed in radically different directions.

Christopher Davenport was converted to Catholicism by a local priest and joined the reformist branch of the Franciscan order, going on to become a professor of theology and, later, chaplain to the wives of both Charles I and Charles II. A man of great intellectual gifts and liberal sensibilities, he was much mourned on many sides of the religious debate when he died in London in 1680.

John, his uncle, became a curate in London after leaving Oxford and was subsequently appointed vicar of St Stephen's Church in Coleman Street, one of the capital's most influential parish churches. A fiery speaker and tireless campaigner, he later became pastor of the English Church in Amsterdam, but his uncompromising and quarrelsome nature quickly led to division, and in 1638 he acquired a patent for a colony in Massachusetts and sailed for the New World, helping to found New Haven colony and Yale University.

John Davenport, the Puritan's Puritan, died in 1670, half a world away from that old English city where he had spent his childhood, alongside his kinsman Christopher. It is tempting to wonder whether, as adults, the two men ever communicated again, or whether all traces of the boyhood friendship they had shared had been lost in those bitter times.

8

AN INDUSTRIOUS REVOLUTION

On a wet morning in April 1765, at a lonely spot on the old road to Kenilworth, troopers Edward Drury and Robert Leslie from Lord Pembroke's Regiment of Dragoons, and a Coventry ribbon weaver, Moses Baker, were hanged for the murder of local farmer Thomas Edwards. The execution was notable for two things. The bodies of the three men would hang in chains at the site for more than forty years, giving the place the name by which it is still known, Gibbet Hill. And before going to the gallows all three had sworn that they would have died in peace had they been able to blow out the brains of the man who had brought them to their end – Alderman John Hewitt.

Hewitt was used to being loathed. A self-appointed guardian of public morals, he was a braggart, supine in the face of those he considered his superiors, but unforgiving to the poor and the lawbreakers who crossed his path.

Born in 1719, from a family long active in Coventry affairs, Hewitt was only in his mid-30s when he became mayor of the city in 1755, but his real ambition was to become a noted thief-taker, like his friend the blind London magistrate Sir John Fielding, half-brother to Henry Fielding, the novelist. In 1756 he petitioned the government to allow him to press petty criminals and the idle poor into the army and navy as the Seven Years' War loomed. Scouring the taverns and flop-houses of Coventry for suitable 'recruits', Hewitt's ruthless pursuit of them made him deeply unpopular. Even army units billeted locally refused to help him, fearing a stain on their reputation.

As a thief-taker Hewitt had his successes, and his activities, set out in his journals, published in 1790, did a lot to galvanise the administration of law and order in Coventry, more than seventy years before the foundation of a city police force. The building of County Hall, opened in March 1785 as one element of improved court and custodial facilities for the city (and county) of Coventry, may well have been a consequence of that.

THE CHANGING CITY

In 1762 New Gate, the old medieval gate covering the road to London, was pulled down. For many years, drivers on the London to Holyhead coaching road had been complaining about how difficult it was to get into Coventry, with its narrow streets and sharp corners, and the old gate must have been quite an obstacle. Within twenty years, four more of the city's historic gates, Spon Gate (said to be the most beautiful of them all), Bishop Gate, Gosford Gate and Greyfriars Gate, had been demolished.

After decades of neglect, Coventry's once awe-inspiring market cross was a casualty too, its upper half removed for being dangerous in 1753, the remainder following in 1771. A smaller Swine's Cross, marking the site of traditional livestock markets at the junction of Bishop Street and Silver Street, was taken down in 1763, while the Drapers Hall in Bayley Lane, a 'dark, gloomy edifice' built just before the Civil War, was replaced by a new building in 1775. But the most radical change to the city's historic streetscape was happening because of the success of its new staple industry – ribbon-weaving. By the 1780s, it was estimated that the trade employed up to 10,000 weavers in the city and its surrounding towns, many of them incomers. Accommodation had to be found for them, and from the middle of the century, modest terraces of houses and courts were being crammed into the gardens and orchards that lay behind the old timber-framed houses lining the streets.

Even so, Coventry had already surrendered its position as the Midlands' biggest and most important city. Birmingham had overtaken it in population around the turn of the century and was already twice the size, its dramatic expansion fuelled by the metal trades that were feeding off the beginnings of the Industrial Revolution.

The contrast between this rapid industrialisation and a craft-based economy like Coventry's was stark, yet there was one major local development from this period that did embrace that rush to new technology.

COVENTRY CANAL

In May 1768 curious crowds gathered in the parish of Foleshill, to the north of the city, to watch a 'porcupine', a giant roller with spikes on it, carving out a huge trench in the ground. They were witnessing the beginnings of the Coventry Canal, a waterway that would eventually link the Warwickshire coalfields with rapidly growing markets they could service and give Coventry's industries their first truly modern route out into the wider world of commerce.

The man with the vision and engineering know-how to make it happen was the great canal engineer James Brindley, hired by the Coventry Canal company in February 1768, but the driving spirits were coal owners like Sir Roger Newdigate of Arbury and Richard Parrott of Hawkesbury, who had actually introduced Brindley to fellow shareholders in the company. Hardly a coincidence, then, that on 10 August 1769 the first two boats making the inaugural journey from Bedworth to the new Bishop Street canal basin should be loaded with coal.

It was to be another eight years before the connection was made with the Oxford Canal, and twenty years before the full 38-mile length of the Coventry Canal would be complete, but the new waterway was immediately profitable and was to remain so for many decades, even after the coming of the railways gave industrialists an even more versatile means of transport to work with.

READ ALL ABOUT IT

News of the canal's coming was announced in the city's first newspaper, *Jopson's Coventry Mercury*, launched back in July 1741 by printer James Jopson from premises in Hay Lane. From the start, Jopson's paper accepted Coventry adverts, but in its early years confined local news to formal notices, announcing rewards for the apprehension of runaway apprentices or the return of chestnut mares stolen from the Park. By the 1760s, however, the paper had been taken over by Jopson's widow Elizabeth and was beginning to raise its sights a little.

Elizabeth, who was advertising her own circulation library by 1764, was one of eleven women operating as printers in Coventry in the second half of the eighteenth century, a remarkably high figure for the time, attributed to the city's non-conformist tolerance towards the female sex. Yet women, so active in Coventry's commercial and social life before the Civil War, had been forced to take a back seat as political divisions came to dominate the city's public life. Only those who were freemen of the city (having served a full apprenticeship or paid a fee to become a freeman) could vote, and women were excluded from that, as from so much else.

SARAH SIDDONS

The great actress, doyenne of the English stage in the last quarter of the century, may well have made her stage debut as a child in Coventry, appearing at a theatre converted by her grandfather, John Ward, from a riding school in the Burges in 1752. As Sarah Kemble, she was back in the city on 24 November 1773 for her wedding to the actor William Siddons in Holy Trinity Church, and in May 1797, at the height of her fame, she returned to appear for a week in four plays at St Mary's Hall.

CAPEL BOND

Coventry never had anything to compare with Birmingham's Lunar Society, although in the 1740s a 'society for gentlemen, for the improvement of learning and natural knowledge' had begun meeting in the Mermaid Tavern. And in the 1750s, a new musical society was staging concerts in St Mary's Hall, featuring the organist and composer Capel Bond.

Born in Gloucester in 1730, Bond was only 19 when he was appointed organist at St Michael's Church, and within three years he had become organist at Holy Trinity as well, probably to boost his rather meagre income. Covering a full timetable of services in both churches must have been an exhausting task, but Bond found time to perform regularly in Birmingham and Wolverhampton, as well as back in Coventry, where in November 1760 he joined the city's new choral society in a performance of Handel's *Messiah*, dedicated to the great man, who had died the previous year. Bond's own legacy as a composer rests on a set of concertos, published in 1766, and on six anthems, written three years later. After many years of ill health, he died in 1790 and is buried in St Bartholomew's Church, Binley.

OLD HABITS

Despite this new flowering of a modest cultural life for Coventry, some old habits died hard. In the second week of September 1780, hundreds fought in the streets in what became known as the Bludgeon Fight, the most violent election in the city's bloody and infamous polling history.

Between 1689 and the municipal reform legislation of 1835, there were forty-eight parliamentary elections in Coventry, and the old Close Corporation wished to control every one of them, by fair means or foul. This time it was supporting two London bankers, standing as Whigs against the sitting Tory MPs, landowner Edward Yeo and John Baker Holroyd, colonel of a regiment of Light Dragoons, billeted locally.

Within half an hour of the polls opening on 9 September, 500 Tory supporters had moved to take possession of the polling booth next to the Mayor's Parlour in Cross Cheaping. Over the coming days, an army of colliers, roughs and prize-fighters recruited by the corporation fought running skirmishes with them that culminated in a pitched battle over possession of that polling booth. The corporation's men were routed and as they sought shelter in St Mary's Hall, the building's medieval stained-glass windows were smashed to fragments as volleys of bricks rained in from their opponents.

After eight days' polling, only ninety-six of nearly 3,000 votes open to city freemen had been cast, and when Parliament re-convened, Coventry was not represented. Another election was called for 29 November, again triggering chaotic and violent scenes in which rival armies marched six abreast through the streets and one man was seen to brandish a sword.

In the uneasy truce that followed, the corporation, knowing that it had lost, secretly enrolled another 150 new 'freemen', many from as far afield as London and Portsmouth. They were later to be dubbed the 'mushroom' voters, as they popped up overnight. The game was up, however. A parliamentary commission stepped in, jailed the city's two sheriffs, Thomas Noxon and Thomas Butler, for ten days for gross dereliction of their duty to see elections fairly contested, and forced through a special Coventry Election Act to tighten up the enrolment of freemen. In the reforming legislation of the 1830s, a special place would be reserved for Coventry as a running sore on the nation's body politic.

Election riot at Coventry. Such scenes were commonplace in the city. (Image courtesy of Culture Coventry (Coventry Archives))

THE BARRACKS

Purely coincidentally, in 1793 the government decided that with war with France looming, it was time to rationalise the stationing of army units throughout the country. Coventry's contribution to that review would be a new cavalry barracks. It was built on the site of the Black Bull, the timber-framed medieval inn on Smithford Street that, as the home of the Onley family, had once played host to Henry VII. Parts of the old building may have been incorporated into the new barracks, but its disappearance from the street scene represented another grievous loss to the city's already diminishing stock of historic buildings.

The first occupants in 1794 were two troops of the 17th Light Dragoons, a regiment that had recently seen service in the American War of Independence, but their stay in Coventry was to be brief.

FOOD RIOTS

On 8 September 1800, food riots broke out in Coventry, inflamed by the appearance in the city of an armed mob of desperate miners from the Bedworth area, intent on 'liberating' food stocks to feed their starving families. As the trouble spread, the mayor read the Riot Act and called upon the 17th Light Dragoons, aided by volunteers from a newly raised Coventry militia, to clear the streets.

The dragoons, it was later claimed, acted with restraint as they cleared angry crowds from Bishop Street, but there were many injuries and possibly even fatalities in what many came to see as a brutal act of repression. Within weeks, the regiment had been withdrawn from Coventry and replaced with infantry soldiers from the 18th (Royal) Irish Regiment of Foot.

THE AFTERMATH

In the wake of the riots, a 'Committee for Bettering the Condition of the Poor' was set up by the mayor, Samuel Whitwell, to sell food at below cost price and review the provision of accommodation and work for the most vulnerable of Coventry's 16,000 citizens. It petitioned Parliament for an act to create 'Guardians of the Poor', in effect every ratepayer in the city who paid more than £20 a year. Their role was to elect eighteen 'Directors of the Poor' to raise money and establish a new 'House of Industry', or workhouse.

What remained of the old Carmelite friary was purchased from its private owners, and by 1804 the inmates of two earlier Houses of Industry, overcrowded and hopelessly inadequate, had been brought together under its roof. This was a

The historic Black Bull Inn. (Image courtesy of Culture Coventry (Coventry Archives))

pioneering move. It was to be sixty years before most towns in England had devised a comparable structure of guardians for the relief of those in poverty.

SERVICING THE STREETS

Coventry was also early in seeking powers to update the provision of essential services like paving, lighting and policing, as well as modernising the water supply. Back in 1762, the corporation had successfully promoted an act of Parliament setting up a body of twenty-two street commissioners with the power to levy a rate for those services. A second piece of legislation, the Coventry Street Act, extended its scope in 1790, and in 1812 a further act was secured, authorising the widening of streets and the creation of new thoroughfares, an improvement desperately needed in a city long notorious for its cramped and crooked streets.

In the years that followed, houses were taken down in Broadgate to widen the market area, and in Much Park Street and Fleet Street, among others, corner buildings were demolished to speed up the flow of coaching traffic.

The most important change, however, was the creation of Hertford Street to bypass the old main road in from the south, the bottleneck that was the winding Warwick Lane. Some of the funding for the street, named after the 2nd Marquess of Hertford, who had recently purchased most of Cheylesmore Park from the Crown, came from an unlikely source.

THE WEAVERS' UNION

With their trade see-sawing wildly, Coventry ribbon weavers, backed by many of the masters, had formed their own Provident Union to try to stabilise wages. In 1819 the union was hauled before the courts and convicted of infringing the

Combination Laws, which prohibited collective bargaining. The fines and costs, amounting to a staggering £16,000, were given to the street commissioners to spend on their road schemes.

The formation of the union followed an astonishing boom in the ribbon trade as the Napoleonic Wars reached their climax. Almost overnight, in 1813, the weavers found themselves in the 'big purl time' in which a sudden fashion for purl-edged ribbons coincided with shortages in skilled labour, forcing up demand. For a couple of years they made the kind of money they could only have dreamed about, but then the fashion died equally suddenly and they were left facing a half-pay apprenticeship system, introduced by the masters to keep pace with demand in times of plenty. This clearly undermined the journeyman weaver, who had served a seven-year apprenticeship and regarded himself as an independent and superior artisan.

In their desperate attempts to sustain prices, Coventry's weavers increasingly found themselves on the wrong side of the law. In August 1821, three ribbon weavers – Edward Cave, Joseph Rice and Thomas Smith – were fined and jailed for intent to compel Philip Harrington, a ribbon manufacturer, to ride backwards on an ass through the streets. This was a traditional punishment inflicted on those who incurred the weavers' displeasure, and it was to be used again the following summer against Amos Carver, a journeyman weaver who had accepted work at lower rates than those agreed. This time twelve weavers were jailed for riot and assault.

A RIVAL TRADE

Watch and clock-making had seemed to make little progress in Coventry in the wake of Samuel Watson's pioneering achievements in the 1680s, but there's evidence of a German watchmaker at work in the city in 1710, and in 1747 Samuel

Vale set up a watch-making firm, giving him the widely recognised accolade of father of the industry in Coventry.

The watch trade never employed the numbers that ribbon-weaving did, but its highly skilled craftsmen clearly felt a notch above their fellow artisans. A parliamentary commission, reporting on the plight of watchmakers in 1817, was told that they had been harder hit by a recession in trade because 'the fraternity thought parish relief dishonourable, since the profession of watchmaker has always been deemed that of a gentleman and the higher order of mechanics'. Watchmakers generally had a higher standard of living, could afford better housing and did not require their wives to work, unlike ribbon weavers, who needed their women folk to help with the demanding business of handloom weaving.

Their pretensions did not always go down well with their fellow artisans, however. During the 'big purl time', it was said, weavers had placed an advert in one of the Coventry newspapers, calling for fifty 'distressed' watchmakers to come and shell peas for them at their regular Saturday night dinner. That said, in June 1821, when the mayor and council decided to make a civic gift to the much-derided Queen Caroline, hapless consort to George IV, it was a Coventry-made watch that they chose.

BUILDING NEW

In the same year, Coventry's first public gasworks was erected in Abbotts Lane, heralding a new phase of city development. In 1828, work started on another major project, the building of a new Holyhead road, bypassing the congested old Spon Street. The following year, construction began on a new church to frame the historic spire of Greyfriars, which had stood alone since the Dissolution. It was to be called Christchurch and would act as a garrison church for the nearby barracks.

By the 1820s the better-off, finding their homes and gardens hemmed in by housing built for the poor, were beginning to move out of Coventry. The city hadn't grown in size for 200 years, fastened in a tight grip by the assiduously defended common lands. There were still at least 1,000 acres surrounding the city over which the freemen were entitled to graze livestock and which could not be built upon.

HILLFIELDS

The first major extension of the city was not built for the wealthy but for that class of independent journeymen weavers who employed others and considered themselves proud members of an ancient and honourable craft. In the late 1820s a new district of sturdy, brick-built houses began to rise on the fields lying between the Swanswell pool and Primrose Hill. Initially known as New Town, the district was later named Hillfields, but if it represented some form of recognition for the journeyman weaver, it wasn't long before he found the proud traditions of his craft under attack.

In late 1831 a mechanic named Josiah Beck introduced steam-powered looms into his premises in New Buildings. At an angry meeting of weavers on 7 November, a crowd of around 200 broke away and attacked Beck's factory, smashing up machines and setting it on fire. Beck himself was roughly handled, and soldiers from the barracks were called in to disperse the crowds.

In the aftermath, three weavers, including a 17-year-old, Alfred Toogood, were sentenced to death for their part in the affray. Only the intervention of Coventry MP Edward Ellice, an influential member of the Whig Government, commuted the death sentences to transportation for life. It was not until the late 1830s that steam power began to get a foothold in the city's ribbon trade, making Coventry one of the last textile manufacturing centres to embrace the new technology.

PARLIAMENTARY REFORM

In June 1832, the Whig government finally managed to get onto the statute books the Parliamentary Reform Act, in which Edward Ellice was a prime mover. It allowed Coventry to keep its two Members of Parliament, but broadened the franchise to all householders living in property worth at least £10 a year. It did nothing, however, to end the way Coventry conducted its parliamentary elections. On 10 December of that year, a date that would long be remembered as the Bloody Tenth, there were pitched battles in the streets as the anti-reform candidates brought in pugilists from Birmingham and hundreds of navvies from Brinklow, where they were working on the Oxford Canal, to disrupt the poll.

The city in due course elected its two pro-reform candidates, including Ellice, but what happened must have influenced a royal commission looking into municipal corporations, sent to Coventry the following June. The Municipal Corporations Act, which came into force on 1 January 1836, swept away the old Close Corporations and many of the ceremonial jobs and structures that went with them, including the Leet. In their place, it created new councils with the power to levy a borough rate and create a new police force. Coventry was to have six wards with six new councillors and two aldermen in each, elected by all male householders of three years' standing.

JOHN CARTER

There was no place for Coventry's veteran town clerk John Carter, a solicitor who, remarkably, had been in office since 1812 and pulled many of the levers of power in the city. Having failed in a long campaign to discredit reform, Carter now took his revenge by acting as legal adviser to communities like Ansty, Keresley and Exhall, which had been part of the old county of Coventry but had long felt they paid higher rates than their Warwickshire equivalents. They took on the new council and won. As a result, the Coventry Boundary Act of 1842 returned them to Warwickshire, and after 391 years, the city no longer had a county to call its own.

THE RAILWAY AGE

In late 1830, Robert Stephenson, son of the legendary George, was appointed engineer to a new railway company, set up to build the London to Birmingham Railway, the first rail link between the capital and a provincial city. Stephenson favoured a route that ran through Coventry, and made the city his headquarters during construction of the Midlands section. When the railway formally opened to passengers on 17 September 1838, Coventry became the closest city to be linked to London by rail, a point not lost on the city's ribbon manufacturers but somehow missed by the railway designers, who gave the place a hopelessly inadequate station that had to be rebuilt almost immediately.

A HOSPITAL FOR THE CITY

On the same day that the new railway opened for business, a meeting at County Hall in Coventry decided on proposals for a new hospital in the city, to replace the dispensaries and workhouse infirmary that had, largely inadequately, served the city's population for many years.

With a donation of £700 from 'an old and influential citizen' named Thomas Wilmot, a house was purchased in Little Park Street. Edward Bourne was appointed the first resident medical officer and the hospital opened its doors in November 1840, comprising one ward with twelve beds in it. In the 1860s, Coventry and Warwickshire Hospital, over-looking the Swanswell, was built to replace it.

CHARLES BRAY

Of the many supporters of the new hospital, none was more committed than Charles Bray, the son of a ribbon manufacturer who had inherited his father's business in 1835. Business did not suit Bray, but he was a passionate social reformer, supporting the city's new Mechanical Institute and starting a working men's club for his own weavers, with reading, dining and smoking rooms, designed to provide an attractive alternative to the pub.

Coventry's first railway station, hopelessly unfit for purpose. (Image courtesy of Culture Coventry (Coventry Archives))

That venture failed, and it's tempting to view the high-minded and restless Bray as a bit of a dilettante and a hypocrite too. Almost a century after his death it was revealed that he kept a second family in Coventry, fathering six children with a woman who was not his wife, the long-suffering, and childless, Caroline.

MARY ANN EVANS

Bray does have one claim to posterity, however: it was his charismatic personality and wide-ranging intellectual circle that drew from Mary Ann Evans, the fiercely intelligent but shy daughter of a Warwickshire land agent, her nom de plume: the great writer, George Eliot.

Mary Ann began attending a school on Warwick Row in Coventry, run by the Franklin sisters, in 1832, the year of the great Reform Act. In 1841 she moved with her father Robert to a house in Foleshill and was introduced to Bray, the captivating brother-in-law of their next-door neighbours.

It was for the *Coventry Herald,* purchased by Charles Bray in 1846 to give himself a platform for his ideas, that Mary Ann wrote her first published work, anonymous reviews and satirical pieces, including a hard-hitting attack on the city's first Chief Constable John Vice, for his alleged connections to a scandal in the butchery trade.

Thirty years later, in *Middlemarch,* her great study of provincial life, Mary Ann recalled those Coventry times. It was the silk-weaving city of the reform years, the coming of the railways and the hospital, against which she set her characters. Rarely has Coventry had a more impressive chronicler.

9

THE AGE OF
MACHINES

In her 1859 novel *Adam Bede*, George Eliot went back to the Coventry she remembered for the courtroom scene in which poor Hetty Sorrel goes on trial for her life. Chapter 43 begins with the words, 'The place fitted up that day as a court of justice was a grand old hall, now destroyed by fire'. As it happens, the guildhall of St Mary was not destroyed by fire, although it came close in the Blitz of November 1940, which gutted the old cathedral, feet away across Bayley Lane. The description that follows is also instantly recognisable today, for the hall is nothing if not timeless.

First constructed in the early 1340s and extensively remodelled in the first quarter of the fifteenth century, it has stood at the heart of Coventry life ever since – seat of government, place of refuge, setting for pomp and circumstance. It has entertained many monarchs and imprisoned just one, Mary Queen of Scots, who was held there for a short time in 1569. It has been a soup kitchen for Victorian weavers, a stage on which the young William Shakespeare performed, and an eighteenth-century election day battlefield, in which rival 'armies' smashed its medieval glass windows with bricks and stones.

Among its surviving treasures is a guild chair, bearing an early carving of an elephant, made by a man who had clearly never seen a real elephant. The greatest glories of arguably England's finest guild hall, however, are reserved for its north wall. Beneath a fifteenth-century traceried window, featuring the images of nine kings in stained glass, is, in George Eliot's words, a 'dozing indistinct dream' of a tapestry, portraying Henry VI and his queen, Margaret of Anjou, with their court. The tapestry, designed for this wall and installed in the early years of the sixteenth century, is now attracting fresh attention as a nationally important work of art.

CHOLERA

On the night of 15 July 1849, two next-door neighbours in Harnall Lane, a mean street of crowded dwellings lying close to the old Leicester road in Coventry, were taken ill with violent stomach pains and diarrhoea. In little more than a week, the sickness claimed ten victims in the street, of whom seven died. Cholera was abroad in Coventry.

Over the next two months, the disease went on to kill 205 people in the city, ranging in age from 9 months to 88 years. Spreading quickly across Coventry's crowded residential districts, it was finally halted by a cholera relief committee, set up in September 1849, which divided the city into three divisions and appointed inspection agents and medical men to each. Within two weeks it effectively had the outbreak under control.

THE RIGHT CONDITIONS

Looking back, the warning signs had been clear for some time. Six years earlier, the Commissioners for the State of

Large Towns had expressed their unease at the quality of Coventry's water supply. In 1845, a highly critical report by civil engineer William Hawkesley branded it 'thoroughly bad and incapable of improvement', and on the back of that he had been commissioned to sink a new well in a corner of Spon End known as Doe Bank and build around it a steam-powered waterworks capable of supplying clean water to some 3,000 people.

The water supply, however, was not the only pressing concern. The appalling state of the city's medieval churchyards, 'crowded pits of putrefaction' as one contemporary called them, had been causing public outrage for many years. In 1844 the council sought an act of Parliament to create a new municipal cemetery on 18 acres of disused quarries close to the London turnpike, and two years later it was laid out to a design by a firm of architects led by Joseph Paxton, who went on to create the Crystal Palace and later became MP for Coventry.

The River Sherbourne, too, had become a serious threat to public health, now little more than a filthy sump passing through a place whose population had more than doubled since the turn of the century. As the new waterworks at Spon End was coming on stream, preparations were being made to clear away the ancient Priory and Bastille mills on the river, opening up the flow of water for a comprehensive new drainage and sewerage scheme, which would take three years to complete.

William Ranger, a superintending inspector of the General Board of Health, was appointed in early 1849 to investigate Coventry as a place where mortality rates from diseases like scarlet fever and typhus (2.6 per cent) exceeded the national average (2.2 per cent). Ranger's view was that chronic over-crowding lay at the heart of Coventry's health problems. He pointed to the fact that the city had 164 courts, alleys and yards, with 1,813 dwellings crammed into them, in which nearly 7,500 people had to live. And he laid the blame for that squarely on the constricting effect of the cherished Lammas and Michaelmas common lands.

OPENING UP

It would be another quarter of a century before the grip of the common lands was finally loosened, but modest extensions to Coventry were already beginning to be made. An 1846 act of Parliament permitted Sir Thomas White's charity to sell land beyond the old suburb of Spon for the development of a new residential district, named Chapelfields, after the medieval leper chapel that had once stood there.

Six years later, a branch of the Freehold Land Society bought 31 acres of farmland in open country to the southwest of the city, divided it into 250 building plots and named it Earlsdon. Like Chapelfields, its target market was the watchmaking fraternity.

JAMES MURRAY

The city centre, too, was experiencing significant change, with ancient landmarks like the Bastille gate and the last vestiges of the medieval bishop's palace being swept away for the construction of Priory Street in the mid-1850s. At the heart of much of it was the young architect James Murray.

Born in Ireland in 1831, Murray was a prodigy, the youngest person ever to be made a Fellow of the Royal Institute of British Architects. His work survives in many places in the UK, but it was in Coventry that he eventually settled and produced some of his finest buildings. Among the highlights were the city's new Corn Exchange, from 1856, and its new School of Art, both sadly now lost, but his Blue Coat School in Priory Row, and the police and court complex he designed as an extension to St Mary's Hall, both still stand.

Murray's life was to be a short one. He died of consumption in October 1863, aged just 31, and is buried in London Road Cemetery. Had he lived longer, his legacy to Coventry

Priory Mill, drawn by Nathaniel Troughton in 1824. (Image courtesy of Culture Coventry (Coventry Archives))

would have accorded him a much more prominent place in the city's story.

LIFE'S A STAGE

The Corn Exchange on Hertford Street may have housed the weekly corn market, but it was also designed as a 'public room' for concerts, lectures and meetings of all kinds – a welcome addition to a city that was still short of places of entertainment. Coventry's first custom-built theatre had been opened back in 1819 by former mayor Sir Skears Rew, who built what came to be known as the Theatre Royal behind the offices of his plumbing and glazing firm in Smithford Street. Within a year or two it was attracting the giants of the London stage, including the Shakespearean actor Edmund Kean, who played Richard III to sell-out audiences in September 1820. Among regular visitors were touring company actors Benjamin and Sarah Terry, who in 1847 became parents to another giant of the English stage, Ellen Terry, born in theatrical digs in nearby Market Street on 27 February of that year.

IRA ALDRIDGE

The Theatre Royal was to earn another distinction that set it apart from all other English theatres of its time. In the spring

James Murray's Corn Exchange of 1856. (Image courtesy of Culture Coventry (Coventry Archives))

of 1828, Rew appointed the American Ira Aldridge, the first black actor to play Othello on the English stage, to be the theatre's next manager.

In a letter to a Coventry newspaper, the first person of colour to run a theatre in Britain promised to improve the fittings and 'make sure that performances started at seven precisely'. But he went further than that. He might have feared, he wrote, that 'unknown and unfriended, I had little claim to public notice, did I not feel that being a foreigner and a stranger are universal passports to British Sympathy'.

Aldridge's tenure at the Theatre Royal only lasted months, before he went back to a stage career that made him something of a celebrity in British and European theatre, but he left one further legacy. In 1828, his presence in Coventry and his vocal support for the abolitionist cause is said to have inspired the people of the city to petition Parliament to abolish slavery.

OTHER PURSUITS

On the morning of 9 August 1849, respectably attired but looking rather more pale than usual, Nuneaton weaver Mary Ball went to the gallows outside the city jail in Cuckoo Lane for poisoning her brutal husband. Hers was the last public execution in Coventry and it was reported that almost 20,000 people were there to witness it. Previously, public executions had been staged on Whitley Common, and its wild expanses were a favourite site for another brutal spectator sport, bare-knuckle prize-fighting.

In the 1840s, Coventry had one of the finest exponents of what was then a less-than-noble art, a Dublin-born former weaver named William Gill. Standing just 5ft 5in and weighing little more than 8 stone, 'Paddy' Gill was nevertheless a clever, two-handed fighter, deceptively powerful and immensely durable. In 1846 he fought for the unofficial lightweight championship of England, emerging after four gruelling hours as the victor.

Gill was to suffer for his gameness – he ended his days in Hatton asylum near Warwick – but he was only one of many Coventry fighters keen to earn money from their fists. Several city pubs served as fighting saloons, and the most prominent was Gill's own headquarters, the Pitts Head in Far Gosford Street, run by a former pugilist named John 'Fatty' Adrian. The pub had another claim to fame. From the 1830s onwards, its stables were used as temporary accommodation for horses running in the Stoke races, then held on open ground beyond Gosford Green.

Another of the city's open spaces, Greyfriars Green, was the venue for the annual Great Fair and Godiva procession, held in June, and in 1848 the appearance of a live elephant, representing Coventry's medieval coat of arms, caused a sensation. The following year, the fair's wild beast contractors, Wombwell's Menagerie, were settling into their quarters the day before the fair when a fight erupted between the two elephants they had brought with them. The keeper was dead drunk, and William Wombwell, the 25-year-old nephew of the proprietor, went into the cage to separate them and was attacked and gored by the animal due to lead the procession next day. Terribly injured, William died two days later and was buried in Coventry's new municipal cemetery. Six years later he was joined in the family grave by his 17-year-old cousin Ellen Bright, known as 'The Lion Queen', who had been mauled to death by a tiger in Chatham.

RIBBONS AND WATCHES

The principal audience for spectacles like these was the working population of the city, the ribbon weavers and the watchmakers, who flocked to public events like the

Great Fair in large numbers. In 1852, Coventry's artisans themselves came under the microscope when the magazine *Household Words* published not one but two lengthy accounts of visits to the city.

The first account, attributed to the writer and journalist Harriet Martineau, was highly critical of the way the ribbon trade was still being conducted in Coventry. No place had more desperately resisted the introduction of steam power, she wrote, and she warned that too many families found themselves totally dependent on the fluctuating fortunes of a single trade. Before it was too late, she urged the men of Coventry to make themselves fit for something other than weaving ribbons.

The second account in *Household Words* came from its editor, Charles Dickens, after a visit to the leading watch-making firm of Rotherhams. He was impressed with the skills he saw on display but contrasted the Coventry way of doing things unfavourably with that of the Swiss, already emerging as major competitors. One reason for the cheapness of Swiss watches, he wrote, was that women worked in the trade there, whereas the men of Coventry would not allow women to be employed as watchmakers.

At the time, these warnings seemed a shade overwrought. By the early 1850s, Coventry had become the dominant centre for watch-making in this country, employing around 2,000 people and overshadowing its two chief rivals, Clerkenwell in London and Prescot near Liverpool. Ribbon-weaving had experienced plenty of hard times but still employed half the city's working population. In 1843, pressure from the ribbon manufacturers had led to the creation of a Coventry School of Design, a distant precursor to the modern Coventry University. The new emphasis on innovative design and quality had paid off. At the Great Exhibition in 1851 a piece of broad silk ribbon, known as the Coventry Ribbon, was widely admired, by the experts as well as the visiting public.

THE CRASH

Harriet Martineau was to be proved right, however. Within a decade, ribbon-weaving as an industry of mass employment was dead in the water. Resentment over the expanding factory system and strikes over piecework rates had weakened the trade, but the mortal blow was the Cobden Treaty, signed in January 1860, which lifted tariffs off many goods imported from France, including ribbons.

In Coventry the trade collapsed almost overnight. A national appeal was launched on the weavers' behalf and raised £40,000. Lord Leigh of Stoneleigh Abbey, a prominent member of a committee of local industrialists and grandees convened to find a replacement for this lost industry, set up his own worsted and woollen mill in the city to offer employment. As an emergency measure, soup kitchens were established in St Mary's Hall, as weaving families literally starved. Those who could do so left Coventry. By 1862, it is estimated, up to 4,000 weavers and their dependants had departed for textile towns further north or emigrated to the United States and the colonies. As a result, the population of Coventry – 41,000 at the 1861 census – had dipped by 3,000 ten years later. The Cobden Treaty spelled disaster for the watch trade too, as a flood of cheaper imports from France and Switzerland gave it challenges that began to appear insurmountable.

FRANCIS SKIDMORE

Salvation for Coventry looked a forlorn hope, but it was to be embodied first in a small, intense character whose diffident personality masked big ambitions. Francis Skidmore was born in Birmingham, the son of a gold and silversmith who shortly afterwards moved his business to Coventry. Young Skidmore served an apprenticeship with his father in

Cross Cheaping, but in 1850 set up in business on his own as an art-metal worker.

Over the next two decades, Skidmore's art-metal company was to become the country's leading specialist in decorative metal, working on some of the most prestigious projects of the age. To the eminent architect Sir George Gilbert Scott, Francis Skidmore was 'the only man in the world to carry out my ideas', and Scott gave him the ultimate sub-contract: fashioning the ironwork for Queen Victoria's extraordinary gothic tribute to her lost husband, the Albert Memorial.

Skidmore's own story ended sadly. His obsessive search for perfection led him to destroy much work-in-progress and the business eventually failed, leaving him to spend his final years in poverty. To Coventry, however, he remained something of a hero. At the height of the ribbon-weaving crisis he had employed out-of-work weavers, and the success of his firm had somehow pointed a new way forward for Coventry as it frantically searched for a future.

JAMES STARLEY

That future came from Sussex, in the shape of a farmer's son with little taste for farming but possessed of an inventive cast of mind that fell little short of genius. James Starley, born in 1830, ran away from the family farm and by his early 20s was working as a gardener for the wealthy marine engineer John Penn in south London. Starley fixed his employer's new-fangled sewing machine when it broke, made one or two important improvements to it, and in 1859 joined the machine's manufacturer Josiah Turner as managing foreman at his works in Holborn.

Two years later, the pair moved their business up to Coventry, chosen because they thought the skills of its watchmakers could be switched to making precision components for the products that their European Sewing Machine Company would be making. After a shaky start, the business proved successful, but an epiphany came in 1868 when Turner's nephew Rowley, their agent in Paris, brought back to Coventry a 'velocipede', pedalling it through the streets from the railway station, to the astonishment of passers-by.

The partners recognised an opportunity when they saw it and sent Rowley back to Paris with orders to sign a contract to import 400 of the machines. They also changed the name of the business to the Coventry Machinists Company to reflect its broadening interests. True to form, Starley immediately began to turn his mind to making improvements to the French machine. In 1871, he designed the Ariel, still regarded as the first true bicycle, and almost casually came up with two inventions that revolutionised transport – the tangential spoke for bicycle wheels and the differential gear, used in motor vehicles ever since. If ever a single individual could be seen as the saviour of a city, the slightly dumpy figure of the man they called the father of the cycle industry was it.

MOVING ON

The crash of the ribbon-weaving industry had an immediate effect on the fabric of Coventry. The number of firms in the business fell from more than eighty to fewer than twenty. Departing weavers left more than 800 houses in the city untenanted, and even the market-leading firm Cash's cancelled phase two of its Hundred Houses cottage factory in Foleshill, having built only forty-eight.

The city was moving on, however. In 1862, Coventry MP Sir Joseph Paxton was one of those who put up cash to build a new and rather handsome School of Art, to replace the 20-year-old School of Design. Five years later, the city built a new market hall to replace the old, hopelessly inadequate structure, which was little more than a shed on brick pillars, and in the same year the Coventry & District Co-operative Society opened for business. At a time when cheating on price and adulterating food was rife, it was instantly successful. Coventry even had its own fire brigade, started by a group of 'local gentlemen' and one of the first in the country. By 1873 it also had a brand new public library, the envy of many other towns.

JOHN GULSON

The man behind the library was John Gulson, a Quaker banker and silk broker who deserves to be remembered as nineteenth-century Coventry's most influential and effective moderniser. A friend to the poor, and to Sir Joseph Paxton, Gulson made many interventions in the life of his native city. He was one of the first to see the desperate need for a hospital in Coventry, gave money to improve the city's water supply, took a leading role in the creation of the School of Art and Technical Institute, and as mayor in the late 1860s was credited with steadying the ship in very rough seas.

The opening of the library – on land he had given – closely followed another milestone for the modernists: the setting up of the Coventry School Board in 1871. Established under legislation to broaden the educational franchise to include all children up to the age of 12, the school board was the first step towards sorting out the jumble of private, charity and grammar schools in the city.

BICYCLING NEWS

James Starley died, much mourned, in 1881, but the industry for which he had laid the foundations was already drawing in innovative engineers and entrepreneurs who could see plenty of opportunities in Coventry. Starley's colleague William Hillman, who had followed him up from London, had set up on his own as a cycle manufacturer in 1876. From Nottingham came Thomas Humber, from London George Singer, from Leicestershire William Herbert and his younger brother Alfred, and from Wolverhampton Daniel Rudge.

From even further afield came Siegfried Bettmann, the son of a Jewish land agent from Nuremburg in Germany, and later on several young Americans, including Oscar Harmer, who was to become the driving force of Alfred Herbert's machine tool firm. Among the prominent names, only the Rileys were from Coventry. They were ribbon manufacturers who had successfully switched trades.

JOHN KEMP STARLEY

Also among those now making Coventry their home was John Kemp Starley, James Starley's nephew, who had joined him in the early 1870s from Walthamstow in Essex. 'J.K.' had set up his own firm with William Sutton in 1877, specifically to develop bicycles that were safer and easier to ride, and in 1885 he had launched a chain-driven machine with two wheels the same size, separated by a diamond frame. He called it the Rover Safety cycle and it was, of course, the bicycle as we know it today. In an inventive history stretching back hundreds of years, Coventry had never given birth to such a future-proofed invention.

News of J.K.'s achievement in 'setting the pattern for the world' was trumpeted by one of the industry's earliest magazines, *The Cyclist*, founded in Coventry in 1878 by William Iliffe, son of a printer and bookseller with premises in Smithford Street. Iliffe later changed its name to *Bicycling News*, and in 1891 launched Coventry's first daily newspaper, the *Midland Daily Telegraph,* which from its beginnings carried a weekly column, 'Cycling Gossip', recording the doings of a trade of which the paper proudly boasted that Coventry was already the centre.

Not every Coventrian was enamoured of the changes to the city that the new industry was bringing with it.

In a letter to Iliffe's paper in November 1891, one local resident wrote:

> Instead of the quiet watch-making, ribbon-weaving place it used to be, Coventry has become a great centre of a new and important industry of a different class, bringing with it large factories, smoking engine stacks, steam whistles, dangerous steam tram engines, a great increase in the artisan working population and over-crowding of the narrow streets and small old dwellings in the centre of the city.

He had a point, but the age of the noisy machines had only just begun.

HARRY LAWSON

Among J.K. Starley's chief rivals in designing a safety cycle – he may have actually got there first but didn't have the company set-up to market it – was a brass turner's son from London named Harry Lawson.

Arriving in Coventry in 1878, Lawson was a highly talented bicycle designer, but his first love was setting up and promoting new companies. He was also a man who could spot a shift in the status quo a very long way away, and from engineering developments he heard about on the Continent, particularly in Germany, he could see that something new and very big was coming. By 1896, in partnership with German-born Frederick Simms, he was in possession of the rights to manufacture Gottlieb Daimler's cars in Britain. On 2 March 1897, the first Coventry-built, Daimler-engined car made its maiden run. Within weeks there were twenty more. The British motor industry, in the shape of the Daimler Motor Company, was spluttering and popping into life.

As the man who ushered in the motoring age, Lawson's future would be considerably more troubled. He may have been a visionary, but he was also a crook, and later served at least one prison sentence for defrauding shareholders, eventually dying forgotten and in poverty in the 1920s.

A TRADE DELEGATION

On a bitterly cold day in December 1899, Daimlers were out in force when Coventry hosted the first foreign trade delegation in its modern history, a visit by Sir Chih-Chen Lo-Feng-Luh, ambassador plenipotentiary of the Chinese empire in Great Britain, Belgium and Italy. Among the firms chosen for his whistle-stop, two-day itinerary were not only Daimler in Sandy Lane and Swift Cycles in Parkside, but the watchmakers Rotherhams in Spon Street and the Stevengraph factory in Cox Street.

The last two were unusual examples of long-established craft businesses that had diversified and survived, against the odds. Rotherhams still made watches but was beginning to manufacture precision instruments for the fledgling machine tool and automobile industries. The Stevengraph Company had been founded by a resourceful and inventive weaver, Thomas Stevens, who in 1862 patented his ideas for making pictures out of silk and had made an international business out of bookmarks and cards.

Another survivor of the ribbon trade, J. and J. Cash, had made a similar sidestep in the 1870s and now manufactured the nation's woven labels. Joseph Cash had at one time attempted to create artificial silk and had failed, but in 1904 there appeared in Coventry a major new employer who could, indeed, make silk that was artificial.

Harry Lawson, visionary and crook. (Image courtesy of Culture
Coventry (Coventry Transport Museum))

COURTAULDS

As the twentieth century dawned, the company was looking
for a site for a new factory in Britain to produce artificial silk,
and they found it in Foleshill, newly drawn into Coventry by
a city boundary extension in 1899. A handy means of transport also presented itself, in the shape of the nearby Coventry
Canal, to distribute the products of this new venture.

The factory opened for business in 1905 and from the outset
it employed women, at first mainly the wives and daughters of

Bedworth miners. By 1913, its largely female workforce had grown to 2,000, but found itself unattractive to the conservative craft unions that had traditionally represented Coventry's artisans. Political change in Coventry, however, was already on its way.

THE LABOUR PARTY

On 6 December 1902, a group of men had gathered at the Alexandra Café on Ford Street to set up a Coventry branch of the Labour Representation Committee, later renamed the Labour Party. Within three years, they had their first seat on a city council still dominated by the 'shopocracy' of publicans, shopkeepers and professional men who had controlled civic affairs since municipal reform in the 1830s.

Coventry's first Labour councillor, watchmaker's son George Poole, was a highly effective and determined campaigner, noted for his work to remove the blot on the city's landscape that was unregulated slaughterhouses. His first focus, however, was on public housing. The census of 1901 had calculated the city's population at just under 70,000, almost double the figure of thirty years before, and the pace was accelerating as its new engineering industries were opening the floodgates to immigration from bigger cities like London and Manchester.

In 1906, Poole was able to persuade the city council to commit itself to a programme of public housing to tackle crippling overcrowding, and the city's first publicly owned housing, aimed at families who could not afford private rents, was a modest terrace of dwellings in Short Street and forty-eight homes in Narrow Lane in Foleshill. Housing, and more particularly the shortage of it, would become a pressing concern for Coventry as the new century beckoned.

10

WAR AND PEACE

On 1 August 1914, Coventry journalist Henry Wilkins began his 'journal of the Great European War' with the words, 'the shadows deepened, the streets were filled with people desirous of hearing the news'. In fact, Britain's declaration of war on Germany was still three days away and on that Saturday evening, up to 25,000 Coventry folk had already left the city, heading for the Bank Holiday highlights of Blackpool or North Wales. In beautiful weather, the prospect of war, however close, was not going to deter Coventry's new industrial working class, still getting used to the idea of a summer holiday away from home.

In the days that followed, preparations for war moved swiftly. Within a week, 1,000 army reservists from Coventry were on their way to their mustering points and huge crowds had lined the streets to cheer the 7th Battalion, Royal Warwickshire Regiment, packed with Coventry men, as it marched through the city centre to the railway station. In an atmosphere of growing war fever, 200 boy scouts were deployed, somewhat improbably, to watch places where 'outrages might be perpetrated', such as the gasworks, sub-stations, canals and telegraph lines. And following the government's hasty introduction of an Aliens Registration Act, more than seventy Coventry citizens, mostly German, had come forward to register with the police.

SIEGFRIED BETTMANN

Among those under pressure because of his German birth was Coventry's mayor, and founder of the Triumph company, Siegfried Bettmann. Ironically, two days before war was declared, Bettmann had been asked by the War Department to convene a meeting of motorcycle manufacturers to discuss the army's requirements in the coming conflict. Over the course of the war his company would supply more than 30,000 motorcycles to the British Army, yet Bettmann's political career as one of the men shaping the Coventry to come was over. He escaped internment in the Isle of Man, the usual fate of 'enemy aliens', but was forced to give up his second year in office as mayor, and his role as one of Coventry's most influential industrialists came to an end. The city would come to regret the loss of his far-seeing and passionate involvement in its affairs.

ENGLAND'S BUSIEST TOWN

As the frantic pace of Coventry's industrial transition to war accelerated, modest-sized, home-grown firms quickly became giants. Before long, a staggering 60,000 people were working in its armaments industries, turning out everything from tiny jewels used in precision instruments to 100-ton naval guns, from the chains used on aircraft cameras to field kitchens, and from seaplane chassis to the explosive bullets used against Zeppelins.

In fields as diverse as the invention of the tank, the development of the aero engine, the creation of a new electrical industry for Britain (the magneto), and the conversion of vehicles for multiple uses, Coventry's name was well to the fore. By 1916, national newspapers were calling it 'The Busiest Town in England'. New housing estates like Stoke Heath were being developed at breakneck speed to accommodate munitions workers, in this case working for the Coventry Ordnance Works, and the population was well on the way to doubling its turn-of-the-century figure of 70,000.

FRANK WHITTLE

Among those 'foreigners' who had already made Coventry their home was engineer Moses Whittle, who had moved from his native Manchester around the turn of the century to work in the cycle industry. By 1907 he had a son, Frank, who would later be credited with an invention that changed the world.

Frank, born in Earlsdon on 1 June 1907, turned out to be the archetype of so many twentieth-century Coventrians – not, perhaps, blessed with the broadest of cultural horizons, but a problem-solver by nature and utterly engineering-obsessed. What set Whittle apart was the flash of genius that enabled him to come up with a method of jet propulsion that worked.

The Whittle family moved to Leamington Spa in 1916, but not before little Frank had experienced his first brush with powered flight, while playing with his friends on Hearsall Common. A plane landed for running repairs to its engine and as it took off again, the updraft blew off his cap. From that moment on, Whittle recalled in his autobiography, all he wanted to do was fly.

CANARY GIRLS

As the war settled into a brutal struggle, dominated by artillery, many Coventry companies switched into munitions, answering the government's call to give the fighting men the ammunition they needed. The biggest was White & Poppe, a modest-scale engine manufacturer that had switched to producing shells, fuses and detonators on its sprawling factory sites in the Holbrook and Whitmore Park areas on the north side of the city.

In the course of the war, White & Poppe employed up to 24,000 munitions workers, the vast majority of them women. They came from all corners of the British Isles and further afield, and they were known as Canary Girls because the dangerous substances they were dealing with turned their skins yellow. Although deaths in the Coventry factories were rare, the long-term effects on their health must have been considerable.

INDUSTRIAL STRIFE

As women, the Canary Girls could not count on much interest from traditional trade unions, and it's an irony that a perceived injustice done to White & Poppe's small male workforce should have brought Coventry's munitions industry to a grinding halt in late 1917.

Signs of growing unrest had been clear early in the year, when a crowd of around 50,000 gathered on Gosford Green to protest at food shortages and apparent profiteering. In November, White & Poppe's management was accused of refusing to negotiate with shop stewards representing their male workforce, and within days, workers at most of the big players in the munitions industry – Hotchkiss, Coventry Ordnance Works, Daimler and Humber among them – had downed tools.

GEORGE HODGKINSON

The strike, fiercely opposed by many in the city and even by Coventry soldiers on the front line, to whom it smacked of treachery, brought to the fore a young shop steward recently arrived in Coventry, who would make a lasting mark on the city over the next fifty years. The son of a Nottingham lace-maker, George Hodgkinson was part idealist, part ruthless backroom operator whose early background of Christian socialism did not stop him becoming the most implacable and scheming of opponents.

On this occasion, as trade union convener at Daimler, he played a major role in finding a compromise to end the strike, but it was to be the start of a fiery political career that gave him a key role on the city council in Coventry's darkest hour in 1940, a lasting reputation as one of the architects of the post-1945 city and, perhaps, an unwanted epithet as the Coventry MP who never was.

PEACE RIOTS

By the time Councillor Joseph Innis Bates, Coventry's mayor, struggled through large crowds to Broadgate on 11 November 1918 to announce that the war was over, the city had lost around 2,600 men. Coventry's engineering industries had done well out of the war, and it might be supposed that prosperity and a universal sense of relief might have led to joyous scenes on 19 July 1919, the day earmarked by the government for peace celebrations. Instead, what started out under sunny skies with children's processions and a peace pageant featuring Lady Godiva, ended with stone-throwing mobs looting shops and battling police in the opening salvos of what became three nights of rioting, the worst in Coventry's modern history.

Over the weekend that followed, the city lurched close to anarchy as street fighting left 100 people injured and dozens of businesses smashed and looted. Only the arrival of substantial police reinforcements from Birmingham and a detachment of soldiers from the Wiltshire Regiment, drafted in from their billets at Radford Aerodrome, finally restored order.

Blamed initially on drink-fuelled hooligans attacking businesses thought to be German-owned, the riots, in truth, stemmed from much deeper feelings of resentment and discontent. It was widely believed that Coventry's celebrations had been monopolised by those who had done well out of the war, while its real heroes faced a chronic shortage of decent housing, poor disability pensions and little prospect of work in factories that had filled their jobs while they were away.

WOMEN AT WORK

Like Courtaulds before them, companies in Coventry's new, post-war industrial sector, electrical engineering, preferred to employ female labour. Women over the age of 30 had been given the vote by the Representation of the People Act in February 1918, and locally there were some small signs of advances for women in Coventry's public as well as industrial life.

The city had acquired its first female tram conductors, police officers and factory supervisors during the war, and in 1919 it also gained its first two women councillors: Ellen Hughes, who stood for Labour in the Stoke ward, and Alice Arnold, who won a seat in the Swanswell ward as a candidate for the independent Workers' Union.

NEEDING HOMES

While many of the women engaged in war work in Coventry had returned to where they'd come from, the city was still a place in which recent immigrants of both genders had invariably been young, placing huge pressures on a housing stock that was already hopelessly inadequate. Many temporary dwellings built for munitions workers had to be pressed into service for young families and had become, by the 1920s, 'drab and cheerless' places. A way had to be found to kick-start better housing.

In May 1925, work began on nearly 140 acres of fields and gardens that had once been common lands at Radford, north of the old city. The Radford garden suburb, as it was known, was the starting point for a council house-building pro- gramme that was to produce more than 2,500 homes in the next fifteen years. The following year, Coventry City Council bought more than 2,200 acres of land from the Stoneleigh estate, south of the city, to develop as largely private hous- ing, and in 1927 a further boundary extension, mainly to the north, dramatically increased the size of the city, from around 4,000 acres to nearly 13,000, adding another 29,000 people to its population.

By permission of " Punch."

THE WAR WORKERS.
"WHAT'S ALL THIS CACKLE ABOUT VOTES AND A NEW REGISTER?"
"DON'T KNOW—OR CARE. WE'RE ALL TOO BUSY JUST NOW."

Last gasp of the chauvinists. The vote for women was coming. (Mark Radford)

CHANGE IS COMING

Fears about the impact that rapid industrialisation was having on Coventry's more venerable fabric had prompted the creation, in 1914, of a city guild to promote public interest in the city's historic buildings and campaign for a proper museum, finally achieved in modest style in 1920.

In 1918 the Church of England had finally bowed to common sense by separating the exploding industrial dynamo of Coventry from the old, rather sleepy diocese of Worcester and making it the focus of a new diocese, converting the huge parish church of St Michael, one of England's largest, into a cathedral.

Two years later the Duke of York, the future King George VI, was in the city to open the new Council House, a long-overdue statement of civic pride begun in 1913 on a site that had been left vacant for a full decade before. Discussions about a separate town hall, which would give Coventry a city centre performance space, came to nothing, but Coventrians did gain a new public park, something else that the city was desperately short of.

Conceived in 1919 as Coventry's memorial to its war dead, the War Memorial Park, formed out of 120 acres of farmland, opened in 1921. Six years later Earl Haig, who had commanded Britain's armies on the Somme, formally unveiled its imposing stone cenotaph.

THE HUNGRY THIRTIES?

The Coventrian of the late 1920s might well hail from somewhere else – there had been branches of associations for Lancastrians, Yorkshiremen and Irishmen, to name just a few, since before the Great War. They were likely to be better paid and younger than the equivalent populations in many other towns, but curiously were less likely to have children.

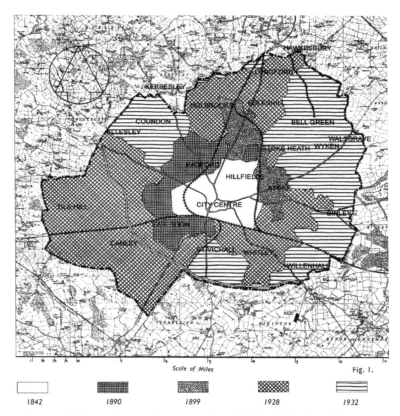

Fig. 1.

| 1842 | 1890 | 1899 | 1928 | 1932 |

A map of Coventry boundary extensions 1847–1932. (David Fry)

This may well have been because many intended to make their stay in Coventry a brief one, returning home before starting a family. Few did, for as the 1930s dawned, they found themselves living in a place of mounting prosperity, in which newcomers really could leap off a train, get a job in the first factory they tried, and if they didn't like it after a day or two, move on to another.

In Coventry, the Hungry Thirties was the decade of the affluent industrial worker. While the unemployment rate in traditional heavy industrial areas like the north-east soared to 25 per cent, in Coventry it remained in the low single figures. In late 1937, Coventry headed the rankings in a new national Purchasing Power Index, designed to calculate the spending power of the public. By the end of the decade, almost one in five Coventrians owned a car, a rate of private vehicle ownership that was only achieved nationally in the 1960s.

BOOM TIMES

Of all the volume carmakers in Britain, only Vauxhall and Ford were not represented in Coventry. The Rootes group and Standard were both based in the city, while for Austin-Morris it was the centre of engine production, first at the former Hotchkiss factory in Gosford Street, acquired by William Morris in 1924, and later at a huge new plant at Courthouse Green.

Blackpool-born William Lyons, who brought his modest sidecar business to Coventry in 1928 and went on to achieve motoring immortality with Jaguar, was only one of a number of entrepreneurs enticed to the city between the wars. In 1938, the *Midland Daily Telegraph* was able to report the construction of twenty new factories and dozens more extensions for companies already in the city, including an extra 300,000 sq. ft for the Daimler company.

JUST LIKE COMMUNITIES

For their workforces, these and other Coventry giants like Alfred Herbert, Courtaulds and GEC had become more like communities in their own right than mere employers. They offered top-class sports facilities (GEC had its own golf course, while Coventry Colliery at Keresley took on two former members of the Yorkshire 2nd XI to bolster its cricket team in the 1930s), a range of welfare benefits and in some cases real educational opportunities.

These companies had a place, too, in the recreational life of those who worked for them. GEC's social club, for instance, enjoyed a membership of more than 4,000, and an annual turnover of £33,000 by 1938. Its company dance hall, the biggest in the city, could entertain more than 1,300 dancers at any one time and boasted a soda and ice cream buffet and an illuminated fountain.

ENGLISH JOURNEY

This was the Coventry that writer and broadcaster J.B. Priestley had observed in his state-of-the-nation study *English Journey* in 1934, writing about 'whole new quarters where the mechanics and the fitters and turners and furnace men live in neat brick rows and drink their beer in gigantic new public houses and take their wives to gigantic new picture houses'.

Priestley was also struck by the ancient city that lay at the heart of this throbbing testament to modernism. 'You peep round a corner and see half-timbered and gabled houses that would do for the second act of Meistersinger,' he wrote. 'I knew it was an old place, but I was surprised to find how much of the past, in soaring stone and carved wood, still remained in the city.'

GOING, GOING

Not for much longer. The pressure of traffic on the old city centre, with its network of medieval streets, had been growing since before the First World War. In 1931, in the first serious attempt to bend that ancient street pattern to the needs of the city of the car, the city council had bulldozed dozens of homes, factories and shops to create Corporation Street, designed to ease congestion around the northern edge of the city centre.

In 1937 they went a step further, demolishing wholesale that Meistersinger landscape of Butcher Row, the Bull Ring, Little Butcher Row and Ironmonger Row to create Trinity Street, another attempt to deal with traffic congestion that now seems like a hideous act of civic vandalism.

NEW RULERS

It was almost the final act of the old 'shopocracy' who had run Coventry for a hundred years, for in the same year the Labour Party took power in the city, giving it its first female mayor, Alice Arnold, and its first city architect and chief planner, the 29-year-old Donald Gibson. His brief was to begin work on the blueprint for a new city centre, but in doing so he clearly began to step on the toes of the long-serving city engineer Ernest Ford, who had been responsible for the creation of Trinity and Corporation Streets and for planning a long-needed bypass for Coventry, the A45, which would open in 1940.

Ford's plans for the city centre envisaged quieter and more intimate places, with broad vistas and grand spaces between Broadgate and the cathedral, but it was Gibson's more radical ideas for a traffic-free shopping centre and sharply delineated development zones that would prevail, even though many of Ford's ideas found their way into the detail of what eventually emerged.

SHADOW FACTORIES

As Gibson and his young team worked on their city centre plans, Coventry was welcoming King George VI, who in

March 1938 came to inspect progress on new shadow factories, including a secret aircraft manufacturing facility at
Whitley and a new aerodrome at Baginton.

The government's idea of building camouflaged industrial units on the edge of cities in the event of war had many
supporters among Coventry's industrialists, notably Alfred
Herbert, William Rootes, the former Singer apprentice whose
giant conglomerate had already swallowed up old Coventry
motoring names like Hillman and Humber, and the Standard
Company's autocratic boss John Black, who still liked to use
his First World War army rank of captain.

Altogether, eight shadow factories were built around
Coventry under the scheme, through which the government paid for and built new plants in return for companies
switching their efforts into war production – principally, in
Coventry's case, aero engines. At the time of the king's visit,
the front-page headlines of the *Midland Daily Telegraph*
reflected the slow but steady march to war. Yet the paper
felt able to assert, in May 1938, that Coventry was 'not
especially exposed to risk of enemy attack' because it lay
in the shadow of Birmingham, a much bigger target, and
being 120 miles inland presented a difficult bombing prop-
osition to a Continental enemy. It was a bizarre notion
– born of First World War thinking – and tragically wrong,
although the first attacks on Coventry did not come from
the expected direction.

THE IRA

At 2.30 p.m. on 25 August 1939, a bomb in the carrier
basket of a bicycle left in Broadgate exploded, killing five
people, including a bride-to-be who was window-shopping
for jewellery, a 15-year-old boy taking his lunch break from
work and the 82-year-old former president of the Coventry
& District Co-operative Society.

The Broadgate bomb was the bloody climax of an IRA campaign of bombings and sabotage launched against Britain earlier in the year, which in Coventry had already led to a string of small-scale attacks on telephone junction boxes, electricity sub-stations and even a waiting room at the city's railway station. It remains the single biggest terrorist attack in Coventry's history, yet it was quickly overshadowed by the declaration of war against Nazi Germany, which followed just nine days later.

TOTAL WAR

Coventry's wartime ordeal tends to be crystallised into the 'Moonlight Sonata' raid of 14 November 1940, the single most concentrated attack on a British city in the Second World War, but there were more than fifty air raids on Coventry, the first of them on 18 August 1940, when high explosives were dropped on nearby residential streets in an attempt to strike at the Standard Motor Company's giant works at Canley. A week later, the Rex in Corporation Street, the ultimate cinema-going experience in Coventry, was blitzed flat on the eve of showing *Gone with the Wind,* fortunately without an audience inside.

The first air raid to inflict fatalities came on 28 August, when bombs dropped on the Hillfields district killed sixteen people. Then, on 14 October, Ford's Hospital, one of the city's most beautiful medieval survivors, was severely damaged by a bomb that killed six elderly female residents and two members of staff.

Although the 14 November raid was unparalleled in its ferocity, the two raids of 8 and 10 April 1941 came close. In the first, the city's Coventry and Warwickshire Hospital suffered repeated direct hits in which more than thirty staff and patients lost their lives. In the second, the church of the Greyfriars, for the second time in its history, lost everything but its spire. Together the two April raids left more than 450 people dead.

MOONLIGHT SONATA

The raid began shortly after 7 p.m. on a brilliant, moonlit November night, so bright that traffic could move around on the roads without lights.The Luftwaffe had gathered more than 400 bombers from airfields all over Europe to deliver a knock-out blow to one of Britain's most important centres of war production, and during eleven hours of bombing dropped 500 tons of high explosive, 30,000 incendiaries and fifty land mines.

Within an hour of the sirens sounding, fire-watchers were reporting 240 fires spread across the city. By 11 p.m., all sources of water to fight the fires had dried up, with the mains shattered and even the Coventry Canal breached and drained. Those trying to save the great medieval church of St Michael's, the city's cathedral, were forced to retreat to save their own lives, and shortly after 1 a.m. the roof fell in.

Alongside St Michael's, the only cathedral to be destroyed by enemy action in the Second World War, Coventry lost its central library and market hall, the new Owen Owen department store and the King's Head hotel, hundreds of shops and public buildings, and sixteenth-century Palace Yard, another great survivor from the city's colourful past.

Coventry's tram system, already considered out-dated, died that night too, while the fire that consumed 15 acres of factory buildings at Daimler's giant Radford plant was one of the biggest of the war in Britain. Around 2,300 houses were completely destroyed, right across the city. The official death toll stands at 554, but that is believed to be a significant underestimate, as many people remained unaccounted for. As dawn broke, hundreds wandered Coventry's streets in a daze, unable to comprehend what had happened. Among them was fire-watcher E.S. Bramwell, who had witnessed the events of that horrifying night at close hand, from the tower of the Council House, right at the heart of the conflagration. In his official log that morning, he wrote:

> Fires still burning, unchecked all around the city centre. The devastation is indescribable. Service personnel make their way slowly over the debris. No-one speaks.
>
> My personal feeling is one of sadness. Then, I recall the starlings trilling a few notes of song as I left the Council House. Did the heat of the fires make them think it was spring, or could this be a message of hope for the future?

THE AFTERMATH

Within two weeks of the 14 November raid, 80 per cent of those thrown out of work by the damage inflicted on factories were back at work. Of the 108 factories left without power after the raids of April 1941, half had had it restored within days.

That said, there is no doubt that Coventry was ill-prepared, at least to begin with, for mass attack from the air. There were not enough fire-watchers to cover every residential street, or enough deep shelters for the population. In the absence of a national fire service, fire crews rushed into the city from other places did not always have compatible equipment that allowed them to hook up to local water supplies, and the idea that the Coventry Canal could be a failsafe back-up for water to fight the fires vanished the moment it was hit, early on in the 14 November raid, and drained.

Coventry's anti-aircraft defences, beefed up only weeks before the November attack, were found wanting too. Of more than 400 aircraft involved, only one raider is known to have crashed that night, and there is no evidence that it was shot down by an anti-aircraft gun defending the city.

Questions were later asked about the city's morale. The fact that at least 50,000 people appear to have left Coventry each night at the height of the bombing to 'sleep out' was unfairly interpreted as a collapse in public morale, ignoring the necessity for many of those involved in vital war work to get at least some sleep under repeated night-time attack.

Critics pointed, too, to some evidence of looting in the wake of the major raids, although most of it concerned theft from meters or machines, not from damaged homes. The criticisms seem to have been sparked as much by the authorities' own panic as anything else, for nothing on this scale had ever happened to a British city before. Hindsight is an unforgiving tool, but Coventry's stoicism and then recovery in the face of unprecedented devastation must be regarded as nothing short of heroic.

11

BOOM AND BEYOND

Other British cities suffered more casualties in bombing raids, but it was Coventry's searing experience that was transmitted around the world as an appalling testament to the brutality of the Nazis. In 1945, confirmation of the city's special status in this country came with the release of a film, *A City Reborn*, made by the Ministry of Information in partnership with Coventry City Council. The government was desperate to avoid the bitter mistakes of 1918 and chose the rebirth of Coventry to epitomise a Brave New Britain, where the returning heroes would have jobs, homes, schools for their children and a comfortable life, free from hard times.

The new city was some time in arriving. A 'Coventry of the Future' exhibition in October 1945 attracted more than 57,000 Coventrians, a fifth of the city's population, to see the plans. But it was to be 1951 before construction began on the cornerstone of Donald Gibson's radical plan – five precinct blocks stretching away from the new square, complete with impressive statue of Lady Godiva, that had replaced the old Broadgate in 1948.

THE STANDARD AGREEMENT

Coventry's industrial economy made the transition from war to peace rather more smoothly, fuelled in part by a remarkable agreement that set the bar of earnings among the city's skilled engineering workers higher than anywhere else in the country. The Standard Agreement, offering a high pay/high productivity package, brought together two unlikely allies, the company's forbidding managing director Sir John Black, and the equally forceful Jack Jones, Coventry District Secretary for the Transport and General Workers' Union.

Liverpool-born Jones had arrived in Coventry in 1938, after service with the International Brigade in the Spanish Civil War. As a young anti-fascist firebrand, he had been waved off to that war by another firebrand with a Coventry connection, the international agitator Tom Mann, one of the pioneers of the trade union movement, who had been born in Longford in 1856 and sent down the nearby pit at the age of 10.

Coventry had first been described as Britain's Detroit during the First World War. Now the expression began to be used again as the city once more became the focus of those in search of a better life, paying the first £5 note in a peace-time weekly wage packet for shop-floor workers. Its rapidly growing population sparked a house-building programme that turned out something like 4,000 houses each year on land brought into the city by boundary extensions in 1928 and 1932. A new generation of edge-of-city estates like Tile Hill and Wood End emerged on virgin farmland.

THE CITY CENTRE

Coventry's central redevelopment was finally coming on stream too. Its pioneering traffic-free shopping precinct, the first in Europe, attracted visitors from far and wide to see the future in action. The Hotel Leofric in Broadgate was described as the finest outside London when it opened in 1955. A new circular market and the beginnings of an innovative ring road followed, and by 1958, Coventry had the Belgrade, the first civic theatre to be built in Britain after the Second World War.

Within two years, it could also boast a new museum and art gallery, named after Sir Alfred Herbert, who had partly funded it. The Herbert's first director was the Ulster poet John Hewitt, whose enthusiasm for his adopted city contrasted sharply with the jaundiced views of his fellow poet and acquaintance, the Coventry-born Philip Larkin.

The son of Coventry's City Treasurer throughout the 1930s, Larkin went on to become in many eyes the greatest English poet of the second half of the twentieth century, but achieved that accolade as a university librarian in Hull.

COVENTRY CATHEDRAL

The crowning glory of the new Coventry was its cathedral, formally consecrated in the presence of the Queen on 25 May 1962, and very quickly regarded as *the* symbol of Britain's recovery from the Second World War. Naturally enough, the people of Coventry had wanted their shattered fourteenth-century cathedral to be rebuilt after 1945, but restrictions on materials and the diversion of skilled labour from the pressing business of putting the country back together had put paid to that.

After winning the international competition to design the new cathedral in 1951, Basil Spence had struggled through political battles and enormous design and construction challenges to create a building that, uniquely, faced north/south, at right angles to its ruined predecessor. In doing so, his decision to commission new work from most of the major artists working in Britain at the time had also created an unrivalled gallery of twentieth-century British art. In the first year after the cathedral's opening, a staggering 4 million people came to see it, and its powerfully expressed dedication to the cause of peace and reconciliation gave Coventry a global profile enjoyed by no other provincial British city.

THE PEACE DIVIDEND

Within hours of the air raid that destroyed the city's four-teenth-century cathedral, the instinctive reactions of two men pointed the way to the future of its twentieth-century successor. Cathedral mason Jock Forbes, looking down into the ruins from the tower, spotted two charred medieval beams lying in the rubble roughly in the shape of a cross, and bound them together. The cathedral's provost, Richard Howard, meanwhile, felt compelled to have the words 'Father Forgive' inscribed on the stone wall behind the altar.

The words were intended to encompass all mankind, not just those who had destroyed the church, and the Charred Cross remains one of the potent symbols of the cathedral's ministry of international reconciliation, alongside the Cross of Nails originally fashioned from medieval roof nails.

The impulse to look forward in friendship and not backwards in revenge found an echo within Coventry's civic leadership. In 1944 they sealed a friendship pact with the Russian city of Stalingrad, the first of its kind in the world, and in 1947 entered into another formal link with the north German city of Kiel.

In 1955, Coventry won an international peace prize from the fledgling Council of Europe as the city that most exemplified the new European ideal of friendship across national boundaries. The following year it established a twinning relationship with another German city, Dresden, and more than sixty-five years on it has twenty-six twin towns, in name at least.

While the cathedral's international ministry of reconciliation and conflict resolution reaches into the darkest corners of the world's killing zones, the ruins of its bombed-out predecessor have become a place in which to reflect on the imag-

Coventry Cathedral in 1975. (Image from the work of Robert Overy, courtesy of Jill Belcham)

ery of peace and commemoration. The profile for Coventry to which Jock Forbes and Richard Howard gave shape, nearly eighty years ago, has lost none of its power to inspire.

PEARL HYDE

In the coronation year of 1953, Queen Elizabeth II had boosted civic pride further by giving Coventry consent by charter to elect a Lord Mayor each year, rather than just a mayor. Four years later, Pearl Hyde became the city's first female Lord Mayor.

The London-born daughter of a publican, Pearl Hyde had arrived in Coventry in the 1920s and had had a 'good war', earning herself a national reputation as a fearless and hard-working organiser for the Women's Voluntary Service, a calming presence amidst the chaos of the Blitz. A larger-than-life character in more ways than one, she had become an influential politician in the post-war years, taking a close interest in housing and family welfare, and might have gone on to greater things. But in April 1963, while on holiday in Scotland, she was killed when her car was in collision with a lorry.

THE BELGRADE THEATRE

A similar fate had befallen Bryan Bailey, first director of the Belgrade Theatre, who died in an accident on the M1 motorway in March 1960, just four months after it had opened. One of the shining lights of his generation in theatre, Bailey created a resident company at the Belgrade, featuring young actors of the calibre of Frank Finlay and Richard Briers, and devised for it an ambitious programme, including the premieres for *Chicken Soup with Barley*, *Roots* and *I'm Talking About Jerusalem*, three plays by an exciting new writer, Arnold Wesker.

Bailey also planted the seeds for a project that was to mature after his death. In 1964 the theatre pioneered 'Theatre in Education', the radical idea of bringing theatre directly into the school classroom. Fifty-five years later, it has spread around the world.

EDUCATION, EDUCATION, EDUCATION

In 1961 the Lanchester College of Technology, a distant descendant of the 1843 school of ribbon design, had opened on a site close to the new cathedral. In the same year the government finally gave the go-ahead to a new university for Coventry, to be built on 200 acres of farmland at Gibbet Hill.

A university promotion committee, led by William, now Lord Rootes, had spent ten years lobbying for a development that in the view of the city's able and influential town clerk, Charles Barratt, was 'the one thing required to make Coventry a great city'.

Even though the initial gift of land came from Coventry, the university was to be named the University of Warwick, an uncomfortable compromise that the headmaster of Bablake School, for one, thought was wrong. 'Why should it not be called Coventry?' he asked, a question that has resounded down the decades since.

Lord Rootes, chosen as Chancellor designate, died before he could take up office, and was succeeded by Lord Radcliffe, the lawyer who had partitioned India, another flawed compromise that had had much more serious consequences. The first students – 340 undergraduates and 90 postgraduates – took up their places in October 1965.

A BOOM YEAR

As 1966 dawned, Coventry folk had plenty to look forward to. There was to be a large new city centre hotel, built almost within touching distance of the north end of the cathedral, and stage four of the pioneering ring road, connecting Spon Street and the Foleshill Road, was scheduled for completion in May.

Two new recreational facilities for the people of the city were also due to be opened that spring. The first was a swimming pool complex in Fairfax Street that boasted the only Olympic-sized competition pool in the Midlands. The second was a new country park at Coombe Abbey, which had been acquired by the city council in late 1964. Later on in the year, the council was planning to open President Kennedy School, the ninth comprehensive school in an authority that had committed itself, perhaps more than any other, to comprehensive education.

HARD LANDING

What was not realised at the time was that 1966 would also be the year in which Coventry's manufacturing output, almost entirely engineering based, would peak. From then on it would start to fall away, and for those who cared to look for it, the first sign was the fate of the city's aircraft industry, clustered around Baginton and Whitley. After a war turning out Lancaster, Whitley and Stirling bombers, peacetime prospects looked bright for a skilled and inventive workforce. In 1947, Armstrong Whitworth Aviation, based at Whitley, had produced the futuristic AW52, the 'Flying Wing'. By the early 1960s, engineers working for its successor at Whitley, Hawker Siddeley Dynamics, were even beginning to think about space satellite design.

The bright hopes of the early years had already given way to uncertainty, however. In 1952, AWA's Apollo, designed and built at Baginton, had failed to measure up to its rival, the Vickers Viscount, and had never made it into production. Later on, Baginton Aerodrome's lack of concrete runways on which to test modern aircraft had forced Hawker Siddeley to acquire an airfield, at Bitteswell near Lutterworth, which could give it that capability. The government never did invest in space satellite design, and in the spring of 1965 Harold Wilson's new administration cancelled three aircraft projects of direct interest to the industry in Coventry – the HS681, the Hawker P1164 and the TSR2. Baginton closed in July of that year and Whitley had followed by October 1968, when it was reported that the aircraft industry in Coventry had lost 11,000 jobs in just five years.

THE CAR INDUSTRY

At a series of Lord Mayor's conferences, convened in the autumn of 1968 to consider the city's future, concerns were expressed that too many of Coventry's industrial eggs now lay in the car-making basket. In an industry long subject to many variables, the warning signs of long-term decline had been apparent for some time.

As early as 1959, it had become clear that Standard and Rootes, the two Coventry-based members of the pre-war Big Six, were heading for trouble. In that year, the Standard Company was taken over by Leyland. This left Harry Ferguson's tractor company, taken on board by John Black in 1946 and housed at the old Standard shadow factory at Banner Lane, to go its own way. By 1967, Rootes had been fully absorbed by the American giant Chrysler, after repeated cash injections from it in the early 1960s.

INDUSTRIAL RELATIONS

Some blamed this decline on the policy of successive governments to direct new industrial development away from cities like Coventry and into industrial areas that were struggling. Others put the responsibility on a local culture of high wages and poor industrial relations for putting off would-be inward investors in the city.

Clearly, there were increasing signs of strife on the factory floor. The old generation of company managers, many of them local men who had risen through the ranks and had something in common with the rank and file, were retiring. Their replacements were younger executives recruited elsewhere who had no loyalty to company traditions, or even, in some cases, to Coventry. By the mid-1970s, only Alfred Herbert of the city's top fifteen employers would have its head office based in Coventry.

The trade unions' trigger-happy response to management aggression, both real and imagined, only made things worse. This gave Coventry an unenviable reputation as a place where people were apt to walk out at the drop of the proverbial hat.

SPORTING LIFE

In the gathering gloom, there was one bright spot – local sport. In 1961, Coventry City, a football club that had been steeped in mediocrity for decades, was suddenly galvanised upwards by a shrewd, energetic and oddly charismatic former footballer, Londoner Jimmy Hill.

In 1967, this master showman, quite happy to plunder cultural references from other worlds, notably the Eton Boating Song, took Coventry City into the First Division in front of more than 50,000 stunned supporters. Off the pitch, Hill made the Sky Blues trailblazers in the world of professional football, pioneering the dedicated match-day programme, a club radio station, special football trains and, later, the all-seater stadium.

By contrast, it was Coventry Rugby Club's adherence to the old values of grit, and a formidable pack, that made it England's premier club by the mid-1960s, its team packed with internationals. The Coventry Bees speedway team, founded in the 1920s, won the British League title in 1968, a precursor to many years as one of the sport's leading clubs, while Coventry Godiva Harriers and the City of Coventry Swimming Club both produced a number of Olympians in that decade.

Coventry's last prominent cricketer had been R.E.S. Wyatt, a former pupil of King Henry VIII School who had captained England in the mid-1930s, but in July 1964, car worker's son Tom Cartwright, one of the cleverest and most accurate bowlers of his generation, won the first of his five Test caps, against Australia. Cartwright, born in a miner's cottage in Alderman's Green and infused with the principled socialism of his parents, should have played for England many more times, but lacked the right background in a game still dominated by class.

HERITAGE IN BUILDINGS

With something of a start, Coventry had discovered in 1966 that it had only thirty-four buildings left dating from before 1700. The Luftwaffe and 'clearances' going back to the 1930s, but reaching their peak in the post-war years, had destroyed literally hundreds more. It was an embarrassment. To save further losses, a townscape scheme was initiated in 1967 to move threatened historic buildings from ancient streets like Much Park Street to a new location in Spon Street. The result was a picturesque collection of late-medieval timber-framed buildings, their impact sadly diminished by the presence of utilitarian tower blocks at either end of the street, and an elevated section of ring road that cut the street in two. Poor Much Park Street, not long before a thoroughfare boasting 600 years of quirky building styles, became largely featureless, its street frontage given over chiefly to grass.

HOUSING ESTATES

By the early 1970s, edge-of-city housing estates in places like Wood End, Stoke Aldermoor and Tile Hill were becoming less attractive as places to live. Experimental building methods like the 'no fines' concrete system had made whole patches of them almost uninhabitable, while communities marooned in a sea of grass, with few of the staple facilities of daily life on hand, were already experiencing social problems.

If the city council hoped that new investment might help, it was in no position to make it happen. A local authority that had been a laboratory for so much social policy in the post-war years, from the smokeless zone to the meals-on-wheels service, was powerless in the face of an accelerating slump.

THE CRISIS DEEPENS

In 1972, redundancies began to accelerate as the oil crisis loomed. Whole chunks of Rolls-Royce's engine business had to be taken into state ownership and its Coventry factories, at Parkside and Ansty, suffered the knock-on effect.

By 1975, the government had been forced to bail out Chrysler to the tune of £162 million, while British Leyland plants were nationalised to save them. At the end of the decade, a study showed, more than 40 per cent of Coventry's working population were dependent on the government for their livelihoods.

It was only going to get worse. The indifference of Margaret Thatcher's government to the plight of industrial cities like Coventry meant that by 1982 the number of British Leyland employees in the city had fallen from 27,000 to 8,000, and the once-great machine tool firm of Alfred Herbert had finally bitten the dust. In 1980 it had been estimated that one in nine of Coventry's workforce was unemployed. Within just a year, that figure had grown to one in six.

Throughout the 1960s, Coventry's population had continued to rise, peaking at 336,000 in the 1971 census. It would dip by a startling 25,000 over the next decade as the city's accelerating economic decline prompted a brain drain among younger, more mobile residents, but the demographic had already triggered a new parliamentary seat for Coventry.

REPRESENTING COVENTRY

The city had emerged from the Second World War with two seats, both held for Labour, oddly enough in the city of the working man, by Oxbridge intellectuals. Richard Crossman represented Coventry East and Maurice Edelman Coventry West, and by 1950 they had been joined by Yorkshire-born schoolteacher Elaine Burton, who won the new seat of Coventry South.

In 1974, the Boundary Commission gave the city a fourth parliamentary seat and renamed them. Crossman had died earlier in the year, but Edelman held on to Coventry North-West until his death in 1975. Former Rootes Group convener George Park became MP for Coventry North-East, Newcastle-born left-winger Audrey Wise took Coventry South-West, and solicitor William Wilson held on to Coventry South-East.

Wilson was one of only a handful of native-born Coventrians to have represented the city in Parliament since the war. As an MP and lawyer, he made immigration his special interest, an appropriate speciality in a place that had, throughout its history, attracted newcomers to put down roots.

COMING TO STAY

In the nineteenth century, local references to immigration from non-white parts of the world are hard to find. The black actor manager Ira Aldridge was in Coventry for a short period in the 1820s, and seventy years later, local newspapers reported the death of Thomas Norbury, originally from the Bahamas, who had settled in Coventry at the age of 28 in the early 1850s.

In the decades before the Second World War, virtually all immigrants to Coventry had been white, mostly from older industrial areas of the UK. In the late 1930s there were also around 2,000 Irish people living and working in the city, and in a mini census taken thirty years later, almost 17,000 people gave their birthplace as Eire. The equivalent figure for the Commonwealth, chiefly the Indian sub-continent, was just over 11,000, roughly similar to those born in the north-west of England and somewhat less than for Scotland.

Generally, Coventry's record on race relations had been a good one. A campaign had to be fought over a colour bar operated by some Coventry working men's clubs in the mid-1960s, but the city's small Pakistan community was the first in the West Midlands to build its own mosque in 1961, and five years later Mohammed Daar started work out on the beat in Coventry – the first ethnic minority policeman in Britain to do so.

MURDER ON THE STREETS

The impression of racial harmony in Coventry was to be shattered in the spring and early summer of 1981. On 18 April, 20-year-old student Satnam Singh Gill was stabbed to death by a gang of white skinheads in a unprovoked attack in the city's Upper Precinct. The weeks of violent racist attacks that followed culminated in the fatal stabbing of Indian doctor Amil Dharry in Earlsdon in early June.

Even before this second murder, shock had given way to a determination to reinforce Coventry's credentials as a place where ethnicity and culture were not provocations, and a march through the city centre at the end of May, organised by Asian community leaders, attracted thousands. It was ambushed by white extremists as it passed the cathedral, and there were confrontations with the police as the march ended, but it made the point. This was, after all, the city of 2-Tone music, which over the past two years had brought black and white youth together in a raucous celebration of British ska.

WHAT COMES NEXT?

It is not an exaggeration to say that the slump of the early 1980s represented the collapse of Coventry as a major manufacturing and engineering centre. On top of it all, the bitter miners' strike in the winter of 1984/85 effectively ended the city's long history as a centre of coal mining, an industry that had brought thousands from all corners of the UK to make Coventry their home.

To its credit, the city council was already taking steps to make sure that the devastating consequences of relying on a single-industry economy would not happen again. To boost Coventry's frankly weak service sector, it was putting a lot of effort into developing a chain of business parks, principally on the southern and eastern edges of the city. Over the next decade or so that move paid off, with a succession of big names from the utility and financial sectors, alongside a sprinkling of relocated government agencies, moving in to take advantage of leafy surroundings in a well-connected location, at a fraction of the cost of doing so in the south-east.

Updating Coventry's ageing city centre shopping offer took a while longer. It wasn't until the early 1990s that major developments arrived in the shape of the West Orchards shopping centre, generally viewed as a modest success, and Cathedral Lanes, widely seen as an ugly failure until its reinvention as a restaurant complex gave it a surprising new lease of life twenty-five years later.

INTO THE NEW CENTURY

As the new millennium dawned, there were grounds for optimism as Coventry's more diversified and steadily improving economy began to attract interest from investors and developers. Significant capital investment was secured for the Herbert Art Gallery and Museum, the Belgrade Theatre and the city's Transport Museum, giving all three a scale and an excitement they should have had decades earlier.

Coventry's Millennium project, the Phoenix Initiative, a clever re-working of landscapes ancient and modern, reacquainted the people of the city with some of the history they had lost, making a real attraction of the city's first cathedral, destroyed by Henry VIII. The Ricoh Arena, opened in 2005, at last gave the city the sort of conferencing and events facility it had always lacked, albeit at arm's length on its northern boundary. In some senses, the Ricoh has given Coventry's sporting life a shot in the arm, staging major international events in several different sports and introducing top-flight club rugby to the city in the shape of the peripatetic Wasps. Yet it has not protected Coventry City football club, FA Cup winners in 1987, from their steady slide out of the Premier League, at one point even dipping to the lowest tier of the English Football League. The city's speedway team, too, dropped out of the top level of their sport after an unseemly wrangle cost them their stadium, while in athletics, swimming and even ice hockey, Coventry's track record has been decidedly patchy of late. Only perhaps Coventry Rugby Club, after a very real brush with extinction, has begun the process of finding its way back to the heights it once enjoyed.

THE RECESSION

Severn Trent's new £60 million operating centre, opened in 2010, appeared to herald a new generation of major job-creating developments in the city centre, but the global recession of 2008, which was unfolding as it was being built, quickly put a block on that.

When Peugeot, Coventry's last volume car manufacturer, closed its Ryton plant in 2006, virtually all of the giant industrial sites that once employed thousands in the city had disappeared. The future of engineering in Coventry now lay with smaller, more specialist companies, many of which had survived the recession remarkably well.

THE UNIVERSITIES

A decade on, the big players in Coventry's economy are now the city's two universities, Warwick and Coventry, with nearly 60,000 students between them and a combined annual budget of around £1 billion. Warwick is firmly anchored in the top ten of British universities, while Coventry is currently the most successful of the 'new' universities. Its £450 million investment programme in both academic buildings and student housing has led to the biggest city centre building boom in Coventry since the 1950s, and for all the fears that accompanied the loss of large-scale manufacturing in the mid-2000s, the city has weathered the latest battering to its economy surprisingly well. While homelessness has risen sharply and council services and family incomes have suffered substantially during the years of austerity, its unemployment rate, in the year up to July 2018, was 4.9 per cent, about the national average.

Figures from the Office for National Statistics show that although Coventry has fewer senior managers and professionals than both regional and national averages, the average weekly wage of male workers is also higher than both. Its population in 2017 was estimated to be just over 360,000, with a string of new communities settling into the city, largely from East Africa, the Middle East and Eastern Europe. Its age profile is also significantly younger than the national average.

CITY OF CULTURE 2021

Both its youth and its diversity were key factors in Coventry's successful bid to become the UK City of Culture in 2021. Not since the 1950s has the city had such an opportunity to place itself in the spotlight of the national gaze. History awaits.

BIBLIOGRAPHY

Bassett, S., *Anglo-Saxon Coventry and its Churches*, Dugdale Society
  Papers 2001.
Bliss Burbidge, F., *Old Coventry and Lady Godiva*, Birmingham
  University Press 1952.
Bottle, T., *Coventry's Forgotten Theatre*, The Badger Press 2004.
Carpenter, C., *Locality and Polity: A Study Of Warwickshire Landed
  Society 1401–1490*, Cambridge University Press 1992.
Chancellor, V. (ed.), *Master and Artisan in Victorian England*, Evelyn,
  Adams & Mackay 1969.
Christiansen, R., *A Regional History of the Railways Of Great Britain
  Vol. 7*, David & Charles 1973.
City Annals – composite version used in *Old Coventry and Lady
  Godiva* (see above).
Clark, P. and P. Slack (eds), *Crisis and Order in English Towns 1500-
  1700*, Routledge & Kegan Paul 1972.
Coss, P., *The Early Records of Medieval Coventry*, Oxford University
  Press 1986.
Coss, P., *Lordship, Knighthood and Locality*, Cambridge University Press 1991.
Coventry Canal Society, *Coventry's Waterway: A City Amenity*, 1972.
Coventry Leet Book (vol. 2) trans. Phillip and Jean Willcox and
  Anthony Divett, Oakleaves Press 2000.
Davis, R.H.C., *The Early History of Coventry*, Dugdale Society Papers, 1976.
Demidowicz, G., *A History of the Blue Coat School and the Lychgate
  Cottages, Coventry*, City of Coventry 2000.
Demidowicz, G., *Buildings of Coventry*, Tempus 2003.
Demidowicz, G. (ed), *Coventry's First Cathedral*, Paul Watkins 1994.
Dodge, J., *Silken Weave: A History of Ribbon Making In Coventry
  from 1700 to 1860*, Herbert Art Gallery and Museum 1988.
Fox, L.,*Coventry's Heritage*, Coventry Evening Telegraph 1945.
Fox, L. (ed.), *Coventry Constables' Presentments*, Dugdale Society 1986.

Goddard, R., *Lordship and Medieval Urbanisation: Coventry 1043–1355*, Royal Historical Society/The Boydell Press 2004.

Gooder, A., *The Black Death in Coventry*, Coventry Historical Association 1998.

Gooder, A., *Criminals, Courts and Conflict*, Coventry City Council 2001.

Harris, M.D., *Life in an Old English Town*, Swan Sonnenschein & Co. 1898.

Harris, M.D. (trans), *The Coventry Leet Book*, Kegan Paul 1907–1913.

Harris, M.D., *The Story of Coventry*, J.M. Dent & Sons 1911.

Hinman, M., *Holy Trinity, Coventry and its Vicars 1264–2007*, Coventry Historical Association 2009.

Holland, C. (ed.), *Coventry and Warwickshire 1914–1919: Local Aspects of The Great War*, Warwickshire Great War Publications 2012.

Hughes, A., *Politics, Society and Civil War in Warwickshire 1620–1660*, Cambridge University Press 1987.

Hughes, A. and R.C. Richardson (ed.), *Coventry and the English Revolution: Town & Countryside in the English Revolution*, Manchester University Press 1992.

Hulton, M., *True as Coventry Blue*, Coventry Historical Association 1995.

Hunt, C., *A Woman of the People: Alice Arnold of Coventry 1881–1955*, Coventry Historical Association 2007.

Hurwich, J., *A Fanatick Town: The Political Influence of Dissenters in Coventry 1660-1720*, Midland History (vol. iv) 1977.

Kimberley, D., *Coventry's Motorcar Heritage*, The History Press 2012.

Lancaster, B. and T. Mason (eds) *Life and Labour in a Twentieth Century City*, University of Warwick 1985.

Lancaster, J., *Godiva Of Coventry*, Coventry Corporation (Paper No. 1) 1967.

Leech, D., *Stability and Change at the End of the Middle Ages in Coventry (1450–1525)*, Midland History (vol. 34) 2009.

Lewis, T., *Moonlight Sonata* Coventry City Council 1990.

Lilley, K., *Urban Design in Medieval Coventry*, Midland History 1998.

Lynes, A., *George Eliot's Coventry*, Coventry Historical Association 1970.

Masterman, J., *Coventry and its Story*, Pitman 1914.

Maycock G., *The Triumph of Siegfried Bettmann*, Coventry Historical Association 2000.

McGrory, D., *A History Of Coventry*, Phillimore 2003.

McSheffrey, S., and N. Tanner (eds), *Lollards Of Coventry 1486–1522*, Royal Historical Society 2003.

Monckton, L. and R. Morris (ed), *Coventry: Medieval Art, Architecture and Archaeology in the City and its Vicinity*, British Archaeological Association 2011.

Munden, A., *The Third Spire: A History Of Christ Church, Coventry*, Coventry Historical Association 1991.

Munden, A., *The Coventry Martyrs*, Herbert Art Gallery and Museum 1997.

Phythian-Adams, C., *Desolation Of A City* Cambridge University Press 1979.

Poole B., *Coventry: Its History and Antiquities* Taunton 1870.

Redknap, B., *Engineering the Development of Coventry*, Coventry Historical Association 2004.

Richardson, K., *Twentieth-Century Coventry*, City of Coventry 1972.

Searby, P., *Coventry Politics in the Age of the Chartists 1836–1848*, Coventry Historical Association 1964.

Smith, A., *The City of Coventry: A Twentieth Century Icon* I.B. Tauris 2006.

Smith, F., *Coventry: Six Hundred Years Of Municipal Life*, City of Coventry 1945.

Soden, I., *Coventry: The Hidden History*, Tempus 2005.

Soden, I., *Ranulf de Blondeville: The First English Hero*, Amberley 2009.

Storey, R. (ed.), *A Shop Steward At Oxford*, University of Warwick 1980.

Tiratsoo, N., *Reconstruction, Affluence and Labour Politics: Coventry 1945–1960*, Routledge 1990.

Tugwood, DT., *The Coventry and Warwickshire Hospital 1838–1948*, The Book Guild 1987.

Victoria County History Of Warwickshire, vols. II and VIII, 1969.

Walters, P., *History In Our Hands*, Coventry Evening Telegraph 1989.

Walters, P., *Amazing But True*, Coventry Evening Telegraph 1997.

Walters, P., *The Story Of Coventry*, The History Press 2013.

Walters, P., *Great War Britain: Remembering Coventry*, The History Press 2016.

Warwickshire Feet Of Fines 1284–1349, Dugdale Society 1939.

Whitley, T.W., *Parliamentary Representation of the City of Coventry*, Curtis & Beamish 1894.

Willcox, P.,*The Bakers' Company Of Coventry*, Coventry Historical Association 1992.

Yates, J., *Pioneers To Power*, Coventry Labour Party 1950.

INDEX